# SEEKING SCENT

The Search and Rescue Stories of Four Special
Brown Dogs & The Secret World They Shared With
Me

A.M. MCGLOON

"I look at my yesterdays for months past,
and find them as good a lot of yesterdays as anybody might want.
I sit there in the firelight and see them all.
The hours that made them were good,
and so were the moments that made the hours.
I have had responsibilities and work, dangers and pleasure,
good friends, and a world without walls to live in."
Beryl Markham


"We make a living by what we get,
we make a life by what we give."
Winston Churchill


"Far and away the best prize that life has to offer
is the chance to work hard at work worth doing."
Theodore Roosevelt

This book is dedicated, first and foremost, to my search and rescue canine partners. Thank you for the memories, the adventures, your trust in me, your grit and your perseverance while seeking out the scent of the missing and the lost. With each search we learned to communicate just a little bit better as you attempted to teach me about your unseen world; so many times, I wish I would have listened a little bit closer. With much love and admiration, here's to you!

K9 Beryl

K9 Connie

K9 Winston

K9 Tollie

And,

To my husband Dave, who supported me, and took care of the dogs left at home while I was away at twice weekly trainings, attending seminars, or on multi-day missions. "Gone girl," as he nicknamed me, is now home. Love you boy.

To all those who believed in me, who challenged me, who guided me with their knowledge and expertise and openly shared their experiences, and who, most importantly, inspired me. Thank you.

To those flankers who were brave, or crazy enough, to support me and the brown dogs over hill and dale or in Winnie's case down into the drainage and back up again. In particular, a shout out to Doug H., Dave K., Ron W., Joe L., Lynda S., Bill O. and Bill C., Lucky L., Denise S., and Kevin H. You always had my back and for that I thank you.

To Josephine County Search & Rescue and the K9 Unit in particular.

To Search and Rescue volunteers and their families everywhere. Do what you do, and do it well, "so that others may live."

# Table of Contents

# Preface

After nearly 15 years as a search and rescue volunteer, what do I remember?

- Driving in the dark, and usually in the rain, to places and addresses otherwise unknown to me.
- Backroads leading to some of the most beautiful places that I've ever seen.
- Dust and mud, lots and lots of dust and mud.
- Faces of fellow searchers, some now starting to fade just as the light fades and dusk slowly descends into night.
- Friendships born of a common passion to serve others.
- Cold uncomfortable nights trying to catch a little shut-eye in my cramped car, a fellow searchers truck, or simply "out there."
- Brush, so much dense brush (manzanita, coastal sorrel and huckleberry) that often the only way through it was to just walk on top of it.
- Twisted vine maple choking the mountain streams, and downfall rife with nature's pongee sticks rooting for you to trip and fall and impale yourself.
- Standing around waiting for an assignment, trying hard to be patient but failing miserably.
- The sound of a jeep horn and the welcoming beam of headlights at the trailhead after hours and hours and miles and miles of being on the trail.

- Soggy sack lunches containing flattened processed cheese mystery meat sandwiches on white bread that tasted almost delicious at the end of a hard day.
- Sparks and toilet paper streaming down the highway when a tyre goes flat on the trailer pulling the loo.
- A steaming hot cup of coffee at the end of a mission.
- Tears. Tears brought on by exhaustion and frustration; tears of sorrow and tears of joy.
- Helicopter airlifts into the Marble Mountains; flying with the United States Coast Guard over the Kalmiopsis Wilderness; and, a little secret kept between a famous local pilot and myself while conducting an aerial search.
- Emotional stresses of broken friendships, all of which are sadly commonplace in organizations populated by driven individuals with unwavering opinions.
- Uncontrollable laughter brought about by a combination of exhaustion and a silly joke no one will remember.
- My faithful dogs. The warmth of their fur after a long day of searching; shivering together under a thin sheet of mylar on a cold unexpected night out; a bond shared of hard work and love that never fades even after they are gone.
- And stories. So many stories, only a fraction of which are contained within these pages; the rest will fade over time except for those small memories, like photographs, that will always remain imbedded within my heart and mind.

----------

All the stories in this small book are true to my best recollection. Many were written only days after a search was declared over, as I found the act of writing cathartic. Some stories have been recreated from my personal mission reports and my memory of the events. All the

*K9 Beryl giving SAR Coordinator Sara Rubrecht a kiss*

individuals are real. I have omitted last names of the search and rescue volunteers I had the pleasure of serving with to protect their privacy. All the map data presented is mine alone taken from my search records.

I wrote this book primarily for myself, in order to keep the memories of some of the most satisfying work I have ever done from fading. One of the first books I ever read on canine search and rescue (*Search Dog Training*, by Sandy Bryson) was filled with stories which inspired me during my time in SAR. I suppose I also hope my stories may inspire others to pursue their passion. SAR is a passion. It's what gets you up in the middle of the night, in the rain and in the cold, to go search for someone you have never met in the hopes of bringing them home safely to their family and to their friends. And you do it for nothing in return, no pay and no accolades; you do it just because there is something deep inside of you that only you recognize. Along your journey, I challenge you to continue to learn, continue to question, believe in your training, and most importantly to listen to your faithful canine partner.

# BERYL

"Dwell on the beauty of life.
Watch the stars, and see yourself running with them."
Marcus Aurelius

# Hunting the Wind: The Making of a Search and Rescue Dog

It was a warm sticky late afternoon in the summer of 2005 when I asked the question, "Do you think a Sussex spaniel would make a good area search dog?" That was the question that I posed to Pluis Davern – a long-time Sussex breeder with years of experience as a professional canine trainer, including search and rescue work – as we sat together on a picnic bench at the conclusion of the first day of our club's annual spaniel hunt test in Mazomanie, Wisconsin. Her response was short but positive, "Sure, with the right Sussex, you bet."

Well, at home I had what I believed was the right Sussex. Beryl, bred by myself and a close friend, possessed the personality I felt would make her an excellent search dog: strong hunt and prey drive, trainability, a love of people, and that seemingly limitless spaniel energy. The preceding summer, I left an almost twenty-year career with the federal government when my husband retired and we moved west to southern Oregon. That first winter in our new home, I joined Josephine County Search and Rescue (SAR) as a ground searcher, something that had interested me ever since taking a mountain rescue training course in college way too many years ago. But I really wanted to be part of the SAR K9 Unit.

Through the winter of 2005-2006, I started going to the K9 Unit's trainings to get a sense of what was involved. I hid for the dogs, I followed along while other handlers worked their dogs and I asked lots and lots of questions. I bought what books were available and consumed everything I could find on K9 SAR. I remember Beryl's first official training day, when she was allowed to come to training and "try-out" for the Unit, like it was yesterday. It was March 2006, the K9 Unit was headed to the mountains for some late season snow training and

Beryl was going to get to do some puppy runaway exercises. Jaws dropped when I took Beryl, who affectionately became known as "little B," out of the car. My training mentor at the time pulled me aside and cautioned me that because of her size (she stood only 14 inches at the withers) she may not make it as a search dog so I should prepare myself in case she washes out of

*Celebrating our first puppy runaway*

the program. Years later we laughed about that first day as Beryl, throughout her career, continued to surprise the doubters and proved that first perceptions are not always what they seemed.

Over the years, I often found myself reciting breed history when asked "What kind of dog is that?" or "She can only search flat park-like settings, right?" My response would usually go something like this: "A Sussex is a working spaniel, a very determined and thorough hunter with great drive, a keen nose, and a special aptitude for thick cover and steep drainages." I would tell people it's those qualities that make her a good match for southern Oregon. My flankers were not always so diplomatic. The area here is still mostly a wild place; thousands of acres of pine forests and steep mountain slopes, which, more often than not, are choked in manzanita, poison oak, and a colorful variety of wild berries that grow with abandon in the near perfect climate.

Beryl loved the puppy runaway game. We progressed slowly and steadily and built a solid foundation over the next year. My mentor, Janet, who ran behind some exceptional bloodhounds, was a kind teacher with a very natural and simple style. Although our paths diverged in later years, I will always be grateful for all that she taught me and in believing in both me and my dogs.

After nearly a year of foundational work, it was time to see how Beryl would perform in her first mock search exercise. In February of 2007 our county SAR team held the first of many mock searches. I loved these exercises as there was no better way to bring all the individual Units together (K9, Mounted, Mountain Rescue, ATV/Snow, Communications, Vehicle, UAV, and the Dive Team) to practice what we trained for. The exercise took place on Stratton Creek, in the Rogue River National Wild and Scenic Area. In subsequent years, this spot became a favorite training area for the K9 Unit and one of the first searches for K9 Tollie occurred along a bend in the road about a half-mile from where the mock search would take place (see the story *One Special Night*). Being February, it was raining with temperatures in the low 40's. I wrote a little story about this mock search in the days following the exercise. Interestingly, writing down my search experiences, became something of a ritual of mine.

----------

The "call" came Friday evening, and I was instructed to arrive at the search location at 0815 the following morning for our briefing. Another canine handler had volunteered to serve as my back-up which was much appreciated. I awoke early in anticipation of what the day would bring. I quickly dressed, made one last check to ensure all my gear was properly stowed in my car, double-checked that I had Beryl's reward (leftover chicken and pork), loaded her in her car crate, and then headed out in the early morning rain. It was about a 50-minute drive from my house to where I was asked to report. From the tiny community of Merlin, the road heads west along the Rogue River towards Hellgate Canyon and just past the canyon is a dirt Bureau of Land Management (BLM) road that veers off to the right; this was my turn. It was then another couple of bumpy miles to base camp and the command post.

Beryl slept comfortably the entire way with an occasional peek out the back window when mom hit a big pothole. After checking in, the search manager gave us our assignment. Beryl was the only member of our K9 Unit to participate in the mock search so I was a bit nervous. Our assignment was to search an approximately 18-acre area for a lost deer hunter. I got all of my gear (must not forget her treats) and then suited her up. She wears an orange search dog vest and an orange collar with a small bell. The bell helps me locate her in heavy brush and also prevents startling a sleeping or feeding bear. I wear a bell as well, just not around my neck.

After studying the map, I decided to work Beryl from south to north along the wide-ridge that bisected the assigned search area. By doing this I was hoping to help her capture any scent that would naturally be flowing uphill in the morning hours. I would work along the western side of the ridge to start and then return along the eastern side of the ridge. Vegetation cover was light as much of the understory had recently been cleared as part of BLM's fire suppression plan. This was a nice change for I usually work Beryl in heavy cover and along steep drainages to take advantage of her breeds strengths.

We commenced our search at approximately 0840 in the still pouring rain. She started working, searching for the lost hunter who she believes has her treats! She quarters ahead of

*Our first mock search exercise*

me while searching for scent. I occasionally give her a hand-signal to have her check to the left or to the right. After only about 8 minutes, her body posture changes. She picks up her pace, stands more alert and I know she is in the scent cone of the lost person. She then races ahead. I quicken my pace as well trying not to trip over down timber and brush. Then, off to my right and about 30 feet away, I hear her bark? I'm a bit puzzled as this is not her trained indication but she must have found something odd and unfamiliar. I look directly at her and see her bark directly at a tree. I see nothing. Then I notice a glint of metal and a camouflaged backpack at the base of the tree and when I finally look up, I notice the lost deer hunter dressed in full camouflage sitting in a treestand about 5 feet off the ground! I call Beryl's name and she races back to me and jumps up and hits my legs with her front paws, and I then ask her to "show-me," and she turns around and races straight back to the lost hunter. The time is 0850. Lots of praises, treats, and puppy kisses! She smells the hunter and shows no sign of fear and is happy to take a treat or two from him as well. I was so proud of her. While in training we set up all kinds of lost person scenarios, but she had never experienced a camouflaged person in a tree stand before.

The exercise, however, was not quite over. I put Beryl's long line on and ask her to "take-us-back-to-camp." She must now lead the entire team back to command. We teach this in case of emergency or just poor visibility and Beryl loves it. She almost gloats with pride as she puts her nose down and takes us directly back into the command area. She continues through the hubbub to where I parked my car and jumps up on the bumper and proudly exclaims "Here it is mom! Treat now, please!" What a good girlie!

----------

By that first week of March, Janet believed Beryl was ready to take her first benchmark evaluation. This is essentially a progress report.

Could my dog work an hour in the field, locate the hider, and independently perform her trained indication behaviour that would signal to me that she had found someone. For Beryl that means doing something called a recall-refind with a jump alert; when she finds the missing person, she should return to me promptly and jump up and hit

me with her front paws and then lead me back to the person she has located. It was snowy cold day on test day. The test site was at a place called Waldo, outside of Cave Junction. The town of Waldo, once the county seat, has now all but disappeared except

*A snowy view of the test area on that cold March day*

for a small cemetery hidden under big pines on the top of a hill. There is a section or two of public land across the highway from the cemetery and behind a locked yellow gate which offered some typical wilderness terrain making it a perfect place to conduct an evaluation. When I arrived, Bob, who was playing the role of the missing person, had already been in place for near an hour. Janet drew the search area out on a map – it was an area of about 40-acres in size and included a ridge, brushy draws, and one steeper drainage with larger trees. Most of the area was covered in tick brush, as we called it, and the ground was rocky indicative of the serpentine soils underfoot. I whispered "search" into Beryl's floppy ear and with that she raced ahead as we headed up toward the ridgeline; we worked together for near that entire

12

hour before she caught scent wafting up from deep down in the drainage where Bob had hunkered down in the trees and brush to find comfort from the snow and cold. Beryl performed her alert perfectly and I looked over at Janet who, with a broad smile, confirmed we had passed our first "test." She called our SAR Coordinator to give her the good news and before I even got home the pager rang with a short line of text congratulating me and "little B."

----------

While most of Beryl's foundation training occurred at the end of Elk Lane, a local road that dead ended adjacent to hundreds of acres of country owned property, in the summer of 2007 I attended my first big seminar out on the plains of South Dakota.

It was June and normally I would have been headed to Wisconsin for the Sussex Spaniel Club of America's annual spaniel hunt test, but this year I was venturing to South Dakota instead for an intense four-day search and rescue canine seminar hosted by the South Dakota Search Dog Association. The group flew in four master trainers for the long weekend. I was excited to be able to meet new canine handlers and train with some exceptional new trainers. Ah, but I am ahead of myself, need to get there first!

I loaded up my little red Subaru and headed downtown to pick up my travel buddy, training mentor, and good friend Janet, and southern

Oregon's only certified trailing dog and B's training buddy, Angie the bloodhound. Knowing this was going to a tight fit for my little Forester even with the "turtle on the top" (my Thule roof case), I asked Janet to pack light so when I pulled into her driveway and saw her suitcase I just had to laugh. It was as big as the "turtle!" So, we repacked in her driveway and finally loaded up the hound in the back. Angie was riding in her "bucket" (the top half of a Vari Kennel nesting in the bottom half) which we managed to fit into the

*K9 Angie & K9 Beryl. Best mates.*

very back of my car while Beryl rode in a wire crate in the center section on the folded down back seats. It was 4'oclock on a Monday afternoon. Somewhere east of Portland while cruising along I-84, Janet asked if I minded driving in the dark; my reply "only when it's raining." Well, west of The Dalles along the Columbia River in the pitch black of an Oregon night weaving our way through road construction, it started to rain, then it started to pour! We smartly stopped for the night.

The next day was mostly uneventful except the check-engine light kept coming on and we learned that Angie was not a fan of the sound or the vibration my car made whenever it rolled over the "your falling asleep now bumps." Road construction in Montana forced us across the bumps numerous times and Angie had finally had enough and, in a panic, she squeezed her massive body across the top of Beryl's crate, scrambled over a pile of luggage and landed with a thud right in Janet's lap. It was raining again and having a bloodhound share the driving compartment at 75 mph is not a good thing. Thank goodness for a nearby freeway exit and doggie sedatives. That night we made it to

Missoula. As we laughed about the day's events and Beryl's hotel room antics (such fun to unroll and toilet paper the room!), Janet said the air smelled like snow. Not in June I thought. Wrong! The next day we found ourselves following the sand truck through blowing sticking snow over the mountains of western Montana. Day three brought us into Gillette, WY and the wonderful hospitality of a dear Sussex owning friend, Susan. She informed us that we had just missed a big tornado outbreak by only a couple of hours. It was great to not have to sleep in a hotel and for the dogs to have some room to run and play.

We woke on day four to a monsoon. The weather was just not cooperating. As we headed along the last stretch of interstate highway before we turned south toward Martin, SD a big neon-sign over the freeway read "Highway 73 CLOSED." That was the road to Martin. Oh no! We stopped at the National Grasslands Visitor Center for some travel advice. We were reassured that the unnamed gravel road, "this one on your map" the nice Ranger pointed at, would lead us directly into Martin. Janet first insisted we stop for emergency rations so at the first opportunity, a funky old and dirty gas station, I dutifully stopped. She ventured in and when she existed through the dirty glass door proudly held up stale buffalo hotdogs in one hand and dangling bags of chips with the other hand. We had only 30 miles to go, 30 miles of South Dakota mud up to the axles. My little car was fishtailing; Janet holding on to the dash for dear life smiling, she was always smiling, laughing and managing to eat a stale buffalo dog all the while having the time of her life. It was an "E" ticket ride that I'll never forget and I hope never to repeat. Martin's blue water tower visible now on the horizon willing us on; we had no choice but to continue for to stop would mean we most assuredly would have become cemented in the mud with no one around to help. We saw but one vehicle in over 30 miles on that crazy but oddly fun muddy road.

We arrived in Martin exhausted as the trip's adrenaline wore off and as soon as we checked into our motel and settled into our room, I poured a strong drink. Martin, from what I could see, was an intersection in the middle of nowhere South Dakota. Training started bright and early the next day. The trainers were Jonni Joyce, Bart Wilson, Janet Wilts, and Chris Weeks. We were to be immersed in air scenting, trailing, and cadaver search work for four intense days. Beryl and I focused on air scent for all four-days as she and I were getting ready to take her first certification test and I wanted to hone her skills and introduce her to new situations. The first two training days were spent out "at Carol's place," a large ranch with grass and corn that went on forever.

I was a bit nervous at first because I wasn't exactly sure how I would be received showing up with a Sussex spaniel, not the most traditional of search dog breeds. I shouldn't have worried as we received a warm welcome and, in fact, there were a wide variety of breeds in attendance: Angie the bloodhound, a wonderful young Weimaraner specializing in cadaver work; a rescued Belgian sheepdog; an Alaskan malamute, a couple of border collies, two English springer spaniels from Oregon; an Australian cattle dog; what looked like a cocker-Labrador mix; a golden retriever, several German shepherd dogs and a Labrador or two rounded out the group. Beryl made me proud during the long weekend. It was hot and humid so most exercises were kept to under 30 minutes. She learned to work in tall prairie grass; this was the first time she and the Belgian sheepdog, who was from Arizona, had experienced working in grassland. The hardest part was actually seeing my dog as the grass was so tall. I worried a bit about the heat and the rattlesnakes, which we had been cautioned to watch and listen for, but she worked her heart out. Her hunt drive was in high gear and the hunting perseverance of the Sussex impressed a couple of doubters. The last two days we were out at "the ranch," a huge spread encompassing a nice variety of terrain – rolling hills, clumps of trees, a meandering stream, and limestone

*K9 Beryl performing her jump alert during a training exercise*

outcrops full of crevices. As we worked our first problem under the trees and along a small creek, Janet, my trainer for the day, commented that she was impressed with how "in tune" I was with my dog, how connected we were. She said, "I think you two will make a good SAR team – about an 8 on a scale of 10." I never forgot that vote of confidence; it was helpful, truthful, and inspiring. When Beryl retired ten years later, I thing she had been correct. We had done good, about an 8 out of 10.

The last exercise of the weekend was a search for two missing persons. I was asked to start working "little B" at the base of a hill and work up toward the ridgeline overlooking a huge depression filled with tall grass. Janet started asking me all about my search plan and trying to divert my attention from my dog who was busy working a rocky outcrop along the ridge we were standing on. I said, "hold on, my dog is in scent." Beryl hung her head over the limestone jumble of rocks on the ridge's rim and came back and gave me a strong jump alert. I raced after her and peered over the edge to see a person hiding in a limestone crevice. Good Job B!! I felt like I had passed some sort of secret test. After high praise and a treat off she went to find the second subject. This was actually a more difficult problem because the person was hiding in the deep grass at the very bottom of the depression. The wind had gone still and the air was thick, hot, and humid and the grass made it feel even hotter; I wondered how she would be able to solve this puzzle but then I witnessed her work the small almost imperceptible dips in the terrain for the presence of scent and she made the find. Watching her work meant she was always teaching me something.

After four days of training, it was time to load everything back into my still mud-caked little car and head west toward home. Our route took us through Yellowstone and Grand Teton National Parks and then down

*Janet rewarding "little B" during a training exercise*

into Idaho, simply a stunningly beautiful drive. I dropped Janet and Angie off in Idaho Falls for their flight home and I headed to Blackfoot to attend a dog show. What was I thinking! We were both exhausted. I decided to head home a day early; only 16 hours to go. I pulled into the driveway and checked the odometer, it read 3,480 miles! Wow.

----------

In September of 2007, we passed our county's 60-acre intermediate level certification. Janet accompanied me to provide support as teammates do, and on the way home, we celebrated by stopping at "Heaven on Earth," a quaint roadside restaurant in Azalea, Oregon along I-5 and famous for their cinnamon rolls. I think they were out of those famous rolls by the time we arrived, but it really didn't matter. We were all smiles and chatting a mile a minute.

The evaluation took place a few miles east of Oakland, Oregon at the historic Kanipe Ranch property, the ranch once part of a greater

18

English Settlement. Evaluations were done "out of county," so they would be as unbiased as possible. This was a tough test of our capabilities and the after-action recommendations were ones I took to heart. I still have the evaluator's report of our test. They wrote:

*"We started at base, at the equestrian area, and walked for an hour to get into the test area. The only problem we encountered was that the area had been "brushed out," and the hawthorn branches were left on the ground. Beryl got some hawthorn stickers in her feet.*

*The actual test area was in timber, with a heavy understory of waist high sword fern and poison-oak, among other things.*

*Ann used good strategy. She did a perimeter search first, to get an idea of the lay of the land. She made sure she knew where she was on the map before starting the actual test.*

*Ann got Beryl into the search area, and started a grid, up the hill toward the ridgeline. Beryl got into some drifting scent, and worked it, but it was not a cone, as Linda was hiding just below the ridgeline. Beryl lost the scent, and again, Ann showed good strategy, as she contoured the area, and moved up the hill and started another grid.*

*Beryl got into Linda's scent cone and worked into the area where Linda was hiding. Due to the brush, there was not much air movement at Beryl's level. In spite of that, she worked the problem out, and found Linda in about 50 minutes. They still had 40 minutes of search time left, not counting breaks, when they made the find.*

*Overall, great job by both handler and dog.*

***Issues***

*The dog faced several issues which could have thrown her off, but didn't. I took my GSD dog, Zeke, with us, on lead. Beryl completely ignored him, and worked as though he wasn't present. She also had to get all the way to Linda without confronting Linda's dogs, which were tied near-by. Beryl took a minute to figure that one out, and worked through that issue very quickly.*

*The day was quite warm, but the dog didn't seem to have much of a problem with it. Ann cooled her in the creek before we started, and after we finished, and she took a spritzer bottle with her, to help keep the dog cool. It shows me that the handler is aware of the issues that the dog faces.*

*The final problem was that the brush was much higher than the dog, and was very thick. Ann let Beryl work at her own pace, and kept checking the air movement at Beryl's level.*

*We had a horse rider following us for part of the search, and a couple of riders in front of us. At one point, we had a helicopter flying overhead, but not at low altitude. There was a fire burning over the next ridge, and the helicopter was associated with that. The air was clear where we were, and not smoky, as the wind was blowing the smoke to the south.*

### Suggestions

*The only things I would suggest are that Ann be provided with a GPS that is more advanced than the one she currently carries. It is very important to be able to see where you have been, and which areas you may need to cover better.*

*The other thing is that Ann may have to be even more strategic in her approach to searching than the average dog handler, due to the physical stature of her dog. Deb W. is a good resource for strategy training. Even though I felt that Ann did very well on her strategy on this test, and has a good grasp of it, I believe it is important that she learn as much as she can in that field. Some of it, however, will only come with experience on actual searches.*

*Linda and I agree that Ann and Beryl are ready to take the State Certification Test, and we will be working to get that scheduled in the next month or two."*

Kathi Flynn, Training Coordinator for Douglas County K-9 SAR and Coos County K-9 SAR

----------

In Oregon, to be fully mission ready and be able to assist in searches statewide, you must be certified to standards set-forth by the Oregon State Sheriffs Association (OSSA). For wilderness air scent dogs this requires you and your canine partner to search an area of 160 acres of both moderate terrain and vegetative cover, and successfully locate a hidden subject. For the evaluation you are allowed four hours to complete the test. The OSSA standards were revised in 2020. The revised standard for wilderness air scent dogs reads: *The test will consist of searching an area of moderate terrain, with light to moderate brush cover, of approximately 60 - 80 acres containing 1 -2 subject(s) in the area, subject(s) are not known to the handler or dog, and locates at least 1 subject (under evaluator discretion). The team must complete the search within 2 hours executing the strategy, making adjustments as appropriate, and being aware of any safety hazards.*

About a month after passing that first level certification test, Beryl and I had an opportunity to test to the OSSA level. Since these testing opportunities didn't come around very often, we jumped on it. But the hot dry October weather and lack of wind conspired and we failed to locate our hidden subject in the required time allowed. No setback goes without its rewards, however, and I learned a great deal from the experience. I knew I really needed to build upon the suggestion that was made to me during our 60-acre evaluation; because Beryl "ranges" as you would expect from a close working gundog – on average between 50 and 150 feet, depending on cover conditions – I realized that for us to be able to be a truly effective search team I needed to be the best handler I could be and try to find reliable ways to "increase her range" and hone my ability to read her specific scent tells. So, throughout the winter, I set up training problems that sharpened my skills as a handler and also encouraged her to range and commit to those first encounters of scent she detected on the wind. I then analyzed her every move. Was that a slight turn of the head as she 'hit' on scent or was it something else? Did her body posture or tail carriage just change? If that was scent, what was her next move? Could I really trust those little body language clues she was providing?

How did I set these training exercise up? Before even arriving at a training location, I would study the map. I would study the terrain. I would study how I believed the wind might be moving scent through the environment. This was the trickiest part but over time it became easier especially when training in known locations as you soon learn and are able to predict the wind flow patterns. I preferred to use open areas where I expected the scent to be carried for considerable distance. The rolling oak hills of Kanipe Ranch were perfect for this so I spent a great deal of that winter training up in Douglas County. I next picked a location for my subject to hide. These needed to be known problems so I could observe Beryl as she searched. Based on wind and terrain, I predicted where I believed she should first encounter scent, where her head might flick in the direction of my hider. When I saw that first "tell" I supported it. I stopped and looked with her; we were, after all, hunting together. I hit mark on my GPS and I took a compass bearing on the exact line her nose was indicating. What was her next move? I silently encouraged her with just a step or turn of my shoulder to "follow up on that tickle of scent" just encountered. She hunted out in front of me as we walked along the heading she just drew on my map. And she would encounter stronger and stronger scent, her confidence growing, and then she found her prize! At the conclusion of the exercise, I studied the maps and wind speeds and noted the distance from the hider when she gave me that first "tell." So, while she remained in my sight during a search, I knew and trusted that a head flick, a change in pace or change in tail carriage meant our subject was 100, 200, 500 feet distant and later learned this could be ½ mile or further.

Little did I know then how significant these skills we learned together would serve me on future missions and also how the same canine "tells" could be applied to my trailing dogs. As a Unit, we also learned how to map what our dogs communicated to us and use these "long-distant alerts" as we called them to help find the missing or lost.

----------

In November of 2007, I got our first taste of what being a mission

*The view west from Squaw Ridge*

ready team was all about. Josephine County SAR had just concluded a search for a reportedly despondent individual. After several days of searching, with no real clues discovered, the mission was officially over. Our SAR coordinator decided, however, that we would search one more day and make it a training exercise. The official search had centered around where the subject's car had been found, just off Forest Service Road 25 (FSR 25), which headed west from Highway 199 up into the mountains to Squaw Ridge. During that initial search, the missing man's dog turned up and searchers strapped a long line on the dog and asked the pup to find his "dad." The dog led searchers on a trek of over nine miles passing Spalding Pond and its small campground, a quaint spot tucked into the mountains west of Squaw Ridge only really known by locals. Guitar pics were found all along the dirt road like a trail of clues leading the dog and searchers to where the 2524 road ended, a breathtaking view overlooking the vast wilderness. This was where our training exercise was to be held, at the end of the road. I was excited to be bringing Beryl and that she and I could do a little searching. It's fun to look back at my first ever search report.

**Thursday, November 1st, Onion Mountain Search**

**Assignment 1**: Beryl & I were assigned to search the slope descending toward the Soldier Creek drainage. This was the area where the search concluded the previous day.

**Search Details**: Clear cool fall day, with light morning frost. At 9:46 am Beryl, myself, and one other searcher entered our search area. The terrain was extremely steep, with thick understory. Beryl showed interest in three areas:

1) 10T 0439865E 4688940N (1031 am)

2) 10T 0439913E 4689016N (1054 am)

3) 10T 0440025E 4689006N (1128 am)

Based on the wind (downslope) and where the search teams had searched the previous day, I believe she was picking up residual scent. She worked through each area of interest thoroughly, but did not alert. It was the last area she showed the most interest. She raced across the slope, through the thick understory, and out of sight; she came back to within about 25 feet at one point and clearly wanted us to follow but her interest died out after a hundred+ yards or so; we circled around as best we could but she showed no further interest. We finally exited the drainage nearly 2 hours 46 minutes later. Arrived back to command at 1245 pm. We traveled approximately 1.4 miles through the search area.

**Difficulties/Hazards**: Very steep terrain, estimate a 45 degree+ slope, and vegetation was very thick. Area was also very damp. Beryl had no difficulties handling the terrain.

**Recommendations for Further Search Efforts**: Nothing at this time.

**Probability of Detection:** 20% (unresponsive); 30% (responsive)

**Assignment 2**: Beryl and I were assigned to search southward along gravel road 760 near where the subject's car had been located. This area had been previously searched by both ground and canine teams on Monday, 29 October.

**Search Details:** We worked along the gravel road (entered search area at 1415) until it became blocked by an earthen berm. There was a good upslope wind so I had Beryl work along the edge of the westside of the gravel road adjacent to Clear Creek drainage. Beryl showed interest at one location along the road near an illegal dumping area. Fresh vehicle tracks indicated possible recent human activity. Beryl went down the slope approximately 75 feet and checked out the area but did not alert. Upon returning to command (exited search area at 1450), I had her recheck the area and she showed no further interest.

**Difficulties/Hazards**: None. Steep terrain on either side of the gravel road.

**Recommendations for Further Search Efforts**: Nothing at this time.

**Probability Of Detection:** 30% (unresponsive); 50% (responsive)

----------

I found every opportunity to train. At least once a week I made an over 100-mile drive to neighboring Douglas County to train with other handers and their dogs. I remember one such day going over one of the four mountain passes between here and there and chuckling to myself that the weather forecasters were so wrong and the Oregon Department of Transportation (ODOT) snowplows stationed at the highest summit were never going to be needed. The sky was grey and the air was cold but the roads were bone dry. I just might have been wrong. By the time I reached Sutherlin the snow was coming down in big thick heavy flakes. I turned promptly around and just cleared the highest pass before the roads were shut. When I got home, one of the Douglas handlers had called to say she had driven out to the training area to see if I was okay and hoped that I had wisely turned around and was safely home. This, of course, was all before cellphones were the norm. By early winter we were on a roll and Beryl and I were working well together, a solid team in the making.

Then a near miss. During one of our county's mock search exercises, my flanker very professionally and silently pulled his sidearm out and asked in a quiet and steady tone "how is little B going to react, we have cougars following us; any chance you can call her back?" "What, where? I don't see them! I have no idea what she will do." Kevin whispered that she was right near where he last spotted them. I spied Beryl up above us on the slope intently smelling something and then she marked over the smell. Well, I guess she has some attitude. Thankfully, she also had a proper recall and I was able to call her back to me. I quickly leashed her up and Kevin quietly radioed our missing subject that we were near and she should stay where she was and we would meet up with her and we would all walk out together. After descending the forested slope, the three of us and Beryl walked along the gravel forest service road back to base, the cats following and observing our every move. A deep sigh of relief but a stark and very real reminder of the potential dangers of training a wilderness search dog.

Then just two weeks later, after a glorious textbook perfect training day, near disaster struck again. I was training up in Douglas County on the same property where Beryl certified just a few months earlier and, as we walked through the large field, we stopped to talk to some of the other SAR personal who were discussing a training exercise. There were two ponies and a large white horse standing nearby. The horse came straight over to Beryl, sniffed her, and then with her right front leg stomped down on Beryl's back right leg. It all happened so fast. Kathy and Linda, the two Douglas County handlers, shoed the horse away as I scooped Beryl into my arms and got her safely out of the field. On the drive home, I believe I was in as much pain as she was. Had Beryl's working life just ended before it had even started? X-ray's confirmed that nothing was broken but it was hard to gauge how much, if any, ligament or other soft tissue damage had occurred. After a couple of days, she was putting some weight back on her leg and then by week's end she was walking on it. But, was the medication masking the pain? I took her off the medication and watched her every step looking for even the smallest signs of pain or stiffness. So far so good but she was on strict rest and relaxation. It's so hard to keep a spaniel still and for a handler to have the patience too not push too fast too soon. Over the entirety of her SAR career, this injury never really faded completely away and I would notice stiffness and soreness after hard days in the field.

Finally, after about a month, I was able to slowly reintroduce some light training exercises. She was happy to be working again. Then I got a call that another testing opportunity was available in early March. Would we be ready? I knew I wasn't going to even attempt the test unless I was certain that Beryl was healed and she wasn't going to be reinjured. I played it day-by-day and by the end of another month I felt she was fit to test. So, in early March 2008, Beryl and I headed back up to the Deschutes National Forest for our OSSA evaluation.

The plan was to test in the same area where we had tested the previous fall but those plans quickly went by the wayside as we encountered roads that became impassable due to the heavy winter snows that had blanketed the Cascade Range. We stopped when we could go no further. Our evaluation site was located at 3,700 feet, the

terrain was sloping and a dense conifer forest covered the area. Forest deadfall, a couple of old clear cuts covered in manzanita, and snow cover ranging from a few inches to over three feet completed the picture before us. The morning had dawned clear, a pleasant 40 degrees, with a light to moderate breeze from the north.

*Improvised testing area*

My search strategy was to search along our western boundary to our southern boundary and then grid in an east-to-west fashion heading northward into the wind. As soon as we began our search, we encountered very tough conditions. Snow level was thigh deep in places and covered hidden obstacles like the twisted and sharp branches of fallen timber and tangled brush. In shaded areas the snow was encrusted with a layer of ice but where the sun had warmed the sparkling surface, we both sank deep into the snow. We reached our southern boundary and then turned eastward on a bearing of 80 degrees. It was rough going; Beryl was frustrated by the deep snow and a couple of times looked at me and said with conflicted eyes, "I'm trying the best I can. This is hard. But I'll find her, let's keep going." Inside, I worried about her leg.

Then, about halfway through our first grid-pass Beryl alerted to the northeast. She momentarily hesitated, held her head high, her body stiff and erect, and pointed in the direction of the scent that she had just caught. I repeated over and over in my head the infamous mantra, "trust your dog, trust your dog." I encouraged her and we headed northeast. We then encountered a "wall" of near impenetrable manzanita covered partially in snowdrifts. Beryl was frantically trying to get through without falling into dead space as she broke through the snow-covered bushes. She looked directly into my eyes and pleaded for me for help, "We need to get through!" I searched for some path, some opening, anything to help but found nothing. I finally just picked Beryl up and like a linebacker pushed through with all my strength. One advantage of having a smaller dog.

A short time later we crossed the tracks of a person, but the footprints were heading in the wrong direction! They were headed southeast taking whoever made them outside the southern boundary of our search area. I asked my evaluator the body size of the subject and was told she was my height and build. I looked at the footprints in the snow and placed my boot next to the impression in the snow and there appeared to be a match. I studied the tracks some more and made the decision to follow. It was a gamble I knew I had to take as the conditions were so difficult that I felt this was our only chance. I had to trust my dog. Beryl had given me her classic natural alert and led us to the tracks; she had to have picked up the fresh scent of our subject. Although hikers and hunters did frequent the area there were no other cars parked anywhere along the road other than ours that day and I knew that subjects make mistakes and don't always hide inside search boundaries. All of this raced through my mind as Beryl worked out ahead of me following the scent trail, stopping to smell the scent as it clung to the bushes and even once or twice putting her nose so deep into the footsteps of what I hoped was our subject that her entire head was submerged under the snow. We had only traveled a short distance, less than 500 feet, when Beryl became

*Beryl locating her subject passing her OSSA Air Scent Evaluation*

extremely animated. To our immediate east was a large conifer thicket, the branches of the trees bending all the way to the ground like the arms of tired old men; the thicket was dark but underneath I could see long-ago fallen trees and other debris littering the forest floor. She began searching in earnest; we were getting close. She worked around the thicket and then she dashed into the darkness. She was gone only a moment when she hurried back to me and I saw the glee in her eyes even before she jumped up on me with her trained alert. "I found someone," she yelled at me silently! I quickly followed her as she led me to the subject who was lying under an old fallen tree covered in a camouflage tarp. At 11:11 am, after just under one hour of searching, Beryl made the find and the test concluded. She became a fully certified wilderness air scent search dog that day, the first Sussex spaniel to be trained and successfully evaluated as a search dog. And my first, but not my last, Sussex to certify for search and rescue work.

Fast forward a week, it's late on a cold Sunday night, and I'm in bed with the beginnings of a terrible cold. My husband comes into the bedroom holding my beeping pager. A lost autistic boy. This is why we have spent countless hours training. I grab my gear, load Beryl up, and off we go on our first official callout.

Certificate of Achievement

Is Awarded to
Ann McGloon and K9 Beryl

Who has successfully completed
Oregon State Sheriffs' Association

K9 Evaluation – Wilderness Area Search

March 8, 2008
Dated

Mack Reid
OPCA Master Trainer

Expires two years after issue

Sara Rubrecht
Josephine County SAR Coordinator

# Clara

One of the largest searches to take place in Oregon happened in Josephine County in the late fall of 2006. The Kim Family search started when co-workers filed a missing person's report in San Francisco, home of the Kim Family. With limited information to narrow down the vast area that needed to be searched it took eight days to locate the family car stuck in heavy snow in the rugged mountains above the Wild and Scenic Rogue River. Katy and her two small children were air lifted to safety but James Kim was still missing. He had left the vehicle to try and walk out and find help for his family. Sadly, his body was located on day ten of the search in the Big Windy drainage. Much has been written on this search and even TV shows and documentaries have been produced so I won't go into any detail here.

I had been in search and rescue less than two years when this tragic event took place and it left a lasting impression on me, just like it did for so many other SAR volunteers. I participated in this search both as a ground and road searcher, as a flanker to Janet and K9 Angie, and in a road security function. At the conclusion of this massive complicated search, Josephine County requested a peer review be conducted to learn what improvements could be made, especially when it came to coordination and communication. There were lessons to be learned. One of the positives that resulted from this review was the formation of a larger regional organization called CORSAR. CORSAR or California Oregon Search and Rescue when it was formed consisted of seven counties in southern Oregon (Josephine, Jackson, Klamath, Douglas, Coos, Curry, and Lake) and two in northern California (Del Norte and Siskiyou). Since then, other organizations, like the Oregon State Police, have been added. CORSAR's primary role is to ensure a smooth process for mutual assist from one county to another. Generally, the way it works is if a search is not concluded in what is called the first operational period – usually the first 12 hours of a search – then additional resources from neighboring counties are called in to assist with fresh resources or specialty teams not available in the requesting county. Starting in 2008, and running for 10 consecutive years, a large Summer-Exercise was held so all the counties could train together. Specialty teams also hosted their own multicounty trainings and Josephine County hosted one of the first regional canine trainings at a beautiful campground called Lone Pine in the spring of 2009.

Over my career in SAR, my dogs and I responded to numerous searches throughout the CORSAR region. This is one such search and one of the first times the CORSAR model was used to request additional resources.

---

The search for Clara took place in early May 2009 just outside the small logging town of Coquille in Coos County at a place called Mountain Homestead. This interesting place, situated on 365 forested acres, and protected by a conservation easement, is *"a cooperative, permaculture-based community of resident land stewards,"* according to an informational brochure we were handed upon arrival. The environment is described this way: *"We are situated within a mixed aged, mixed species forest with plenty of wildlife. There are many trails and connection to 15 square miles of forested habitat as well as a beautiful city reservoir which serves as out private swimming hole. We recently purchased 35 acres of adjacent land."* This was a big place and Clara, who was 71 years old and suffering from dementia had been missing for two days.

Coos County Search and Rescue had been searching all day prior to fresh teams arriving from several counties. Upon arrival, I was suddenly thrown into a coordination position for the canine teams; there were teams from Coos, Josephine, Jackson, and Klamath present. It felt a bit

*Coordinating canine assignments*

awkward being asked to coordinate canine assignments for another county's search when I knew they had experienced canine handlers who could perform the same task, but command had asked so I did my utmost best. The only map available was a hand drawn map. I conferred with one of the homestead's residents and got everybody out searching in short order. Beryl and I then donned our gear and started our search efforts as well.

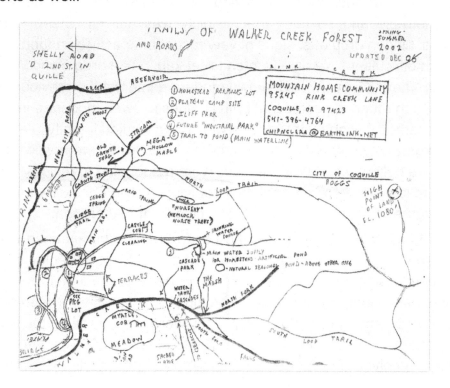

During our initial search efforts that morning, I teamed up with Cathy, from Coos County, and her dog, K9 Lucky. We had three support personnel with us – Abigail and Sam from Coos and Joe from Josephine County. We also had with us two of the homesteads' residents acting as guides, Chip and Dermot, to help us navigate through the thick brush. Our search area wasn't terribly large, roughly 40 acres, but coastal searching is always tough going. Drainages are steep and the vegetation is customarily thick and impenetrable. Sword fern, vine maple, salal, and downed timber meant we were often on our hands and knees in the mud. At least it wasn't raining. Temperatures were moderate, in the 50's, there was little wind, and only a soft drizzle when we entered the woods at 1020 in the morning.

Our search strategy that morning was to attempt to grid search from west to east; the sword fern and other vegetation was at times impenetrable and so thick that visibility was difficult. Steep muddy slopes, hidden drop offs, signs of very recent bear activity, added to the search difficulties. We also wanted to reexamine an area along Walker Creek where K9 Lucky had shown moderate interest the previous day. My search report indicates that both canines showed moderate interest in the same location on this day as well. Beryl worked intently in a small drainage and we noted a footprint in the mud. When we reviewed the map, we believed that both the dogs were responding to residual scent trapped in a small scent pool within low lying Walker Creek. By the time we returned to base it was after two o'clock in the afternoon.

As I loaded Beryl back into the car for some much-needed rest, I noticed she was limping just a little bit. I decided not to deploy her on another assignment unless absolutely necessary. Janet and her bloodhound Angie were still out searching, doing another sweep along the west perimeter of the property. They were working along the Ridge trail and Angie was picking up scent. It was almost 4:30 in the afternoon when I received a radio call from Janet asking if I could please bring

Beryl over to the ridge and work her along the trail as well. There was a nice upslope breeze coming from far below where Rink Creek cascaded down the hillside. The slope down to the creek was crazy steep covered in thick sword fern and heavy forest. Joe accompanied Beryl and I as we headed over to the Ridge trail to meet up with Janet and Angie. Angie bumped into Beryl who snarfed at her; yup, she was hurting a bit as these two were best buddies. I told Janet we would try but I wasn't sure Beryl could actually navigate the slope if she picked up any scent from below.

As I worked Beryl along the Ridge trail, her behavior changed and she alerted twice to scent wafting up from below. Her leg was cramping again so I called in another air scent team that could navigate the terrain before us. K9 Slate and Micki from Jackson County were still on site and were available to assist. Her dog also responded to the scent with significant changes of behaviour. Neither of our dogs, however, were able to descend the slope and follow up on what their senses were communicating to them. We all returned to command to report formally our efforts and to ask permission to search from the bridge over Rink Creek upstream to below where the dogs were indicating. It was now well after 5 pm.

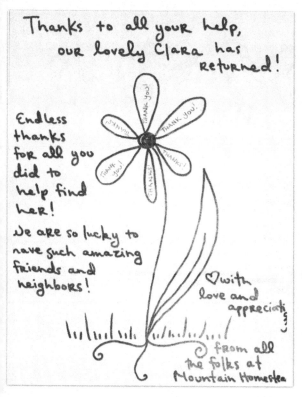

Thanks to all your help, our lovely Clara has Returned!

Endless thanks for all you did to help find her!

We are so lucky to have such amazing friends and neighbors!

THANK YOU! THANK YOU! THANK YOU! THANK YOU! THANK YOU!

♡ with love and appreciation from all the folks at Mountain Homestead

35

During our debriefing, a call came in that Clara had been located. Unknown to us at the time, family and friends had been monitoring the communication between the canine teams and base while we were up on the Ridge trail reporting what we were witnessing. They understood and immediately had started searching Rink Creek immediately below the Ridge trail. And this is exactly where Clara was located. She was along the bank of Rink Creek in the direction K9 Angie had indicated and the air scent dogs had alerted; the air scent alerts were between 735 – 850 feet from Clara.

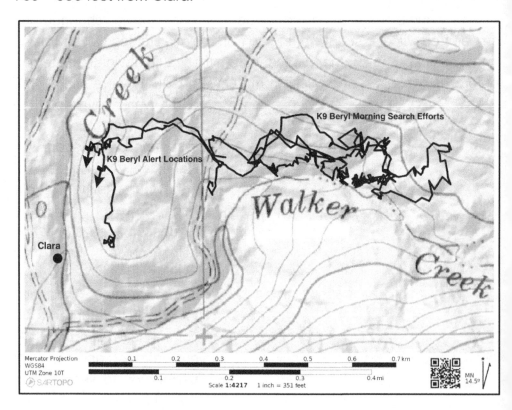

# Anniversary

In the spring of 2010 Beryl and I were gearing up to recertify as a wilderness air scent team but we were also training in wilderness human remains detection (HRD) with plans to attempt certification over that summer. When this search occurred, we were not yet "official," but we were asked to assist with the search efforts. Less than a month later, in June, we passed our wilderness HRD evaluation and recertified in wilderness air scent.

----------

May 23rd 2010. Sunday's search was a first for me, an airplane crash. We got the call at around 10 pm Saturday night that search teams were needed for the following day to search the site where a Socata single-engine aircraft went down in the mountains south of the small town of Happy Camp in northern California. The pilot, 84-year-old Alonzo "Lonie" Edward Mullin of Medford, while presumed to be deceased had not yet been located. According to news reports at the time, Mullin reportedly had taken off alone from Palm Springs, California, at 8:30 am Saturday. He reported having trouble descending through the clouds in Northern California at 1:30 pm. The aircraft then dropped off radar and lost radio contact over the small town of Happy Camp. The Siskiyou County Sheriff's Office also received several calls at about the same time from residents reporting a possible plane crash south of town in an area known as Titus Ridge. We learned that he was a World War II Veteran who had served in the Army and had survived the Battle of the Bulge and then served as an infantry scout as the Germans retreated across Europe. Maybe, somehow, he had survived the crash.

In order to travel down to Happy Camp and arrive in time for the morning briefing, I was up at the darkest hour of the night and was at our SAR house in Merlin in time for a 0400 departure. We were six in total plus two dogs, Beryl and Josie, a black Labrador. I shoved all of my gear and "little B" into Randy's four-wheel drive truck. Beryl road in the hard-shelled covered back of the truck in her crate while Josie stretched out in the jump seat of the cab. It was a 3-hour journey that took us down Interstate 5, over the Siskiyou Summit into California, and then onto winding State Route 96 to the little town of Happy Camp along the Klamath River. For us locals, this was actually the long way around since the more direct route to Happy Camp was still impassable due to late spring snowfall. After meeting up with additional crews at the Forest Service Ranger Station in Happy Camp, we started out again on another 45-minute drive along a series of forest service roads before we finally made the last turn along a very muddy single-track road to the top of a ridge which overlooked what seemed like the world. The Klamath River below, looking so small, cutting its way westward through the mountain canyons to finally empty into the Pacific.

The search area was divided into an upper slope and a lower slope which was bisected and accessed by an overgrown logging road. The slope had obviously been logged years ago and was now choked with brush 20-feet tall and "reprod" so tightly planted that it was a near impenetrable wall of wet green foliage.

The assignment given to us was to search the upper debris field first from the ridgeline down to the small overgrown skid road before dropping further down the mountain and toward where some of the larger pieces of aircraft had been located the previous day by a helicopter that had overflown the site. There was a helicopter on site this day as well which was going to try to rotor wash the brush down to search for more debris. Aircraft debris was spread out on the entire slope that was probably 50 to 55 degrees and in some places more extreme. Randy and I were asked to bring our dogs with us and work them but the primary search strategy was a that of a tight grid line search from the top of the ridge to the river, some 5,100 ground feet below. As I got Beryl ready for the day a Forest Service employee whispered to one of the Josephine County searchers "what on earth is a dog like that going to do here, in this terrain?" Joe told me later that he suggested to the man that he try and follow us through the rugged terrain, if he could that is.

As the line of searchers from several counties hiked single file along a small steep trail to the mountain top, we passed personal items entangled in the brush and strewn along the trail: a ball cap, a flight jacket, and shards of metal, plexiglass, and fiberglass. Once at the top, we lined up across the extent of the debris field and started down, searching as best we could on the steep slope. There was so much fiberglass and plexiglass, a white towel hanging on a branch, a gasket from somewhere on the aircraft. I heard Randy over the radio say he had located the log book, another searcher called in an empty flight procedure manual; the vegetation was so thick that at times I was on my hands and knees or just holding on to branches trying to keep from sliding down the muddy slope and trying to keep up with Beryl who was

easily navigating through the thick brush; she was animated and clearly interested in the area as she sniffed intensely at any debris we located. At the top of the cutbank as we emerged from the brush and above the skid road bisecting the slope, Beryl stopped and lifted her head into the upslope wind and pawed the

*Overlooking the crash site*

ground, part of her trained human remains final response. "Below, further down the slope," she told me. How far, I had absolutely no idea.

The search managers then faced a tough decision as the clock raced toward the afternoon. It was clear that they were very nervous about sending anyone further down the slope. It was getting late and they were rightly worried about safety and being able to get searchers back up and out before nightfall. All sorts of ideas were floated about. How about having us search all the way to the river which was still at least 4,500 ground feet below (a 2,000-foot vertical drop) and then having a raft pick us up and ferry us across the river to Highway 96? Who was short-haul certified? Was there another helicopter available to assist? A head-count was done on who even wanted to attempt the effort; most of us raised our hands, heck that was why we were there.

I called my husband on a borrowed cellphone to let him know how things were going and to see if he had any ideas that I could share with the Search Managers. My husband started flying in his teens and has thousands of hours under his belt in all types of aircraft, I wanted to hear his thoughts. He relayed that often the pilot would be thrust forward into the instrument panel and that the best chance we had of locating him was to find the front section of the aircraft. I shared the information with the SAR Managers but suspect that they had already drawn the same conclusions.

Finally, it was decided that two small teams would hike down toward the large sections of debris and search around the immediate vicinity. The K9 teams and the remainder of the ground searchers were all put on "standby;" a tough assignment when you want to help, search, do what you were trained to do. So, in the afternoon Randy and I and couple other searchers sat on the ridge overlooking a forest of bright green just listening to the progress of the search over the radio as the two teams ventured further downhill.

As a searcher it was so very frustrating just sitting at the top of the mountain while others were searching. I was never good, and am still not, at sitting idling around and waiting. I like to keep moving. I decided to take Beryl for a walk along one of the muddy tracks that led to the backside of the ridge; we were joined by another searcher who also needed to keep moving. An old piece of logging equipment sat idly along the track and Beryl raced over to investigate. I noticed her putting her head down and sniffing intently at something white. Oh, it's a one of the laminated cards from the flight procedural manual. It reads "Normal Flight Procedures," then we spot another card "Stalls," then another "Involuntary Spin," then another and with each card the flight emergency just got worse. Then Beryl alerts to a white handkerchief hanging on a branch; she sniffs and then paws madly at the ground. We head back to base to report our findings and then find ourselves sitting again above the ridge listening to radio traffic from below.

Debris descriptions and UTM coordinates would break the radio silence every so often. But as the crews got closer to the main portion of the aircraft, the calls were coming in almost right after each other. Aircraft debris reporting turned into personal items: a shoe was located, a stuffed teddy-bear with flight goggles, a wallet, a pair of twisted pants with personal effects. Finally, the radio call came in that the front of the aircraft had been located but no sign of Mr. Mullin or even any sign of blood. Could he have been ejected out as the plane tore itself apart? It was getting late and the search crews didn't have time to search any longer, so they started the long climb back up.

After the teams were safely back up, a debrief was held. One of the personal items brought back up from below was a small appointment notebook. One of the search managers opened it up to the day's date and written on the page was one clearly legible word. That word read "Anniversary."

Alonzo "Lonie" Edward Mullin's body was discovered on Tuesday, near what remained of the aircraft's engine at the bottom of the debris field, four days after the crash of his Socata aircraft in the mountains of northern California.

# Outside of Prineville: Learning About the Long-Distance Alert

The day after little Zoey was found in Curry County *(see the story Starry Starry Night)*, I was on my way to Prineville, Oregon, with another canine handler and his dog from our Unit, for a weekend of training hosted by High Desert Search Dogs and Crook County SAR. This was in mid-March of 2010. Since conceivably we could be requested to respond to searches throughout the State of Oregon, this was a perfect opportunity to get acquainted with searching in the high desert. The other Josephine County K9 Unit team members chose to remain at the coast for additional coastal training hosted by Coos and Douglas County K9 Units.

The search adrenaline still had me a bit pumped and the drive went by quickly as we rolled into Prineville late on a Friday afternoon. The calendar may have said spring but the thermometer read 24 degrees at 0800 as we gathered at the makeshift command post Saturday morning where FSR's 27 and 33 intersected in the Ochoco National Forest. Two handlers and their canines had braved the frigid night air and camped in their vehicles; it was a plus for the rest of us because they had a very welcoming roaring fire going when we arrived. There were five search areas to choose from for that day's wilderness air scent training. I chose area 5. Area 5 was a roughly 160-acre parcel of pine forest and sage brush, bisected by a ridgeline, and included a seasonal creek all at an elevation of around 4,000 feet. My hider left command and drove up the road ahead of us to find just the perfect hiding spot. Caroline, a handler from Lane County, served as my flanker. Neither Caroline nor I had any idea where our training subject was going to hide so this would be what is known as a double-blind exercise. Every time we train. we hopefully learn something, and on this day the lesson learned proved to be one of the most valuable and useful to date. A lesson that would serve myself and others well in the not-too-distant future. I witnessed something I refer to as "the long-distance alert."

The wind was blowing briskly from the southwest and as the sun heated the high desert, I expected some morning upslope winds as well especially on the more exposed south or eastern facing slopes. My search strategy was to first work the forested northwestern flanks of the two small butte-like hills that formed a mostly north-south running ridge that bisected my search area; when reaching a small creek that served as my southern-boundary I would then return north on the east side of the ridge through more open terrain. Just past the one-hour mark into our search, Beryl gave me a hard jump alert. I was surprised because I hadn't seen her show me all the normal behaviours that would indicate she had actually found someone. I still responded, however, with the customary "show me" and Beryl spun around and then just circled the immediate area with her head held high trying desperately to pinpoint the hider who was nowhere nearby. There was no question she had detected human scent but she was unable to follow the scent to the customary conclusion. Some in the trade might call this a "false alert," but I strongly disagree. A true false alert happens in the absence of a trained odor. She had encountered human scent so I call this, simply, communication.

I marked the alert location on my GPS (point #714) and took a compass bearing on the wind direction (west by southwest); this is something that should always be practiced in training so it becomes reflexive during an actual search. The scent information your canine partner has just communicated to you could become the vital piece of information that leads to a successful search outcome. The forest below us was thick with quite a bit of downfall and although Beryl showed little interest directly downslope of where she had alerted, I still felt it needed to be checked so we did just that. We ventured down the slope and made a wide circle through the thick forest well below the ridge. As we began our counterclockwise circle along the slope, Beryl ranged out ahead and started "pulling" us to the southwest but that was leading us outside our designated search area. Just as we were about to complete the loop, on a northeast heading now, Beryl gave me another hard alert and I marked it immediately on my GPS (point #715; wind west by southwest). What was happening?

Caroline and I studied the map and we had two theories: 1) our hider was on the east side of the ridge and the scent was looping over the top; or 2) our hider was further to the southwest and outside the search area. We decided to test out the looping theory first. It was a bust. As we crossed over the ridge to the grass and sagebrush filled east side, Beryl showed no interest at all. The only excitement was a rabbit darting across the landscape, thankfully Beryl wasn't interested in the antics of a silly rabbit. We continued all the way to a small seasonal creek and then decided to head south and then due west and play out theory two. Bingo!

Our hider was outside the search area. He was directly upwind of where Beryl alerted twice and at roughly the same elevation; he said he had wandered up and then down trying to find a good hiding spot and also noting his GPS was acting up. How far away was Beryl when she alerted to his presence? I was surprised when I measured it at between 2,000 – 2,400 feet (almost a half-mile)! I probably wouldn't have believed it if she hadn't alerted twice along the same "line;" and, she never had lied to me. She was right. I believe some of our earlier training, where I had worked on increasing her effective range, had contributed to this beneficial form of dog to handler communication.

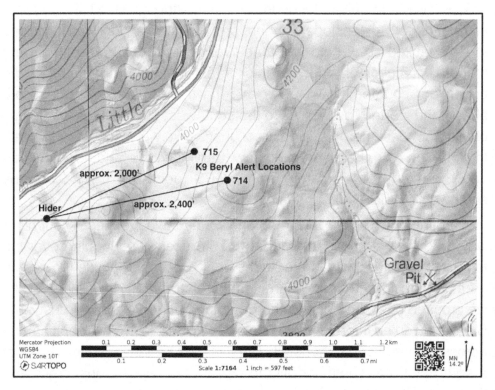

After suggesting our hider move back into the search area, Caroline ran her gorgeous solid black German shepherd on what turned out to be a near identical scenario. She also experienced a similar long-distance alert.

I found this stuff fascinating; it was data analysis, something I had spent a career doing while working in the Central Intelligence Agency's Crime and Narcotics Center. One of intelligence projects I had been responsible for was analyzing the flight data from the US State Department's funded aerial drug eradication program in Colombia. Contracted pilots flew T-65 "Thrush" crop spaying aircraft over both the opium poppy and coca growing areas releasing a glyphosate mixture to kill the illicit narcotics crops below all the while the aircraft recorded a variety of data as the herbicide was dispensed. It was my job to sift through the reams and reams of data and convert the calculation of herbicide dispensed to actual crops destroyed. Let's just say my findings didn't always agree with the US Government's public claims.

*Suiting "B" up with the Astro 220*

So, when Garmin released the first dog tracking collar, the Astro-220, I immediately purchased one. I was probably one of the first handlers in southern Oregon to begin tracking my dog's movements during training and on searches, something that is now commonplace. I then put on my analyst hat and studied the dog track GPS data exploring and learning as much as I could about what my dog was doing and why. Just like I had done with the "Thrush" data, I coupled my dog's track data with imagery and maps. I then studied the terrain, wind direction, and how this might all effect scent dispersion and ultimately to learn how my dog was reacting and using the wind and the terrain to do what came so naturally to them.

What I like to tell my students today, is that we can study scent dynamics (and I think every handler should) but the real teachers, the true masters are our dogs. I learned an incredibly valuable lesson that day in the Ochoco Mountains. Over the course of my SAR career, both my air scent girl and my trailing dogs exhibited long-distance alert behaviour both in trainings and during actual deployments. In fact, it was something I would see again just four months later in some of the wildest country I ever searched in – the upper reaches of the Sixes River in Curry County.

# Sixes River Search

The origin for the name Sixes stems from the Indian word Sik-ses-tine, meaning 'people by the far north country.' Gold miners shortened it to Sikhs, which they knew meant 'friend' in the Chinook jargon. I personally didn't find the wildness of the region all that friendly.

I was tired. For a good portion of Monday, July 26th 2010, I had been searching with K9 Connie in the city of Ashland for a man with early onset dementia. Connie was Beryl's dam and was my first certified mantrailing dog. I started training her in February of 2008 while Beryl was recovering from her near disastrous encounter with the big white horse and Connie earned her OSSA trailing certification in June 2009. It was nice having both an air scent and a mantrailing dog; plus, Connie loved all the Public Relations Events while Beryl wasn't all that interested or always suitable.

So, instead of a nice quiet day around the house, I rose at 0300 to meet up with my fellow searchers for a search over at the coast. In total there were nine Josephine County searchers and three canines that met up at the SAR house to organize gear and then set off in a mixed caravan of personal rigs and official vehicles. We were met along Highway 101 by a Curry County Sheriff's Deputy who led us the 22 or so miles up into the coastal mountains. After about 15 miles, the paved road turned to gravel, the usual gray dust blowing up behind the vehicles and covering and permeating everything. Signs of recent logging were everywhere as the road climbed higher and higher; massive swaths of forest laid bare in a logging technique known as clear cutting rendering the slopes bare, full of slash, and downright ugly.

We finally reached "base," which was nothing more than a wide crossroads of logging roads radiating off a central hub in different directions similar to the face of a compass. Teams were briefed on their various assignments. As reported by Scott Graves, a staff writer for the Curry Pilot newspaper, the background to the search went something like this.

*"At 10:20 a.m. Monday, the Curry County Sheriff's Office received a call from 27-year-old Robert Nodine reporting that his uncle, William Cox, and his father, Robert Nodine Sr.,62, were missing in the upper area of Sixes River near Star Mountain.*

*Details were sketchy late Tuesday but, according to Sheriff Bishop, Nodine said he left his father and uncle on Sunday to retrieve their car and meet them the next day at Sixes River Campground. The two men were going to hike down the south fork of the river to the campground. When they didn't show Monday morning, the younger Robert Nodine called authorities.*

*Bishop described the area as being about 27 miles east of the intersection of Highway 101 and Sixes River Road. "This is nasty territory. One slip and there's a 200-foot fall in many places," he said.*

*Based on information provided by Nodine, Bishop activated the Curry County Search and Rescue team to find Nodine's father and uncle. On Monday afternoon, a search team found the father, who had managed to hike out of the Sixes River ravine to a nearby dirt road. He said the path down the river had been blocked by a waterfall. The uncle, Bishop said, may have tried to get around the waterfall and continue hiking down the river toward the campground."*

Since the father had climbed out of the drainage on the north slope. Could the missing gentleman, William Cox, have tried to do the same? The three Josephine K9 teams were asked to search along the north slope of Rusty Creek and all the way down to the creek and try and find out. The only map we were given was a xerox copy of the region from an Atlas. As someone with a background in maps, this wasn't too satisfying or reassuring.

49

Rusty Creek had several currently active mining claims in addition to old paths and roads that were hand cut (I overheard someone say by the Chinese) into the mountain over a hundred years ago when the area was rich in gold. To describe the terrain as difficult does not do it justice nor adequately describe what teams were to encounter. Forested and often scree covered slopes of 60-70 degrees; some very old roads and trails choked with vegetation and downfall making travelling through the area extremely difficult. The area also had a rich and coloured history that could send a shiver up the spine of even the hardiest of men.

The Indians that once inhabited the area called them "Swalalahist" or "Indian Devils," large man-like beasts that lived in caves in the far upper reaches of the Sixes River.

*"One of the most remote stories of the Southwestern Oregon country is the legend of the South Sixes River ape man. The folklore of the very early day miners of the Sixes gold field is spiced with tales of an uncanny creature resembling a huge monkey. Most of those that had ever come in contact with old Saucer Eyes, as he was called, were shocked by his sudden appearance and surprised at his rapid "getaway." It was a saying among the miners that one could be on the constant lookout for the old scamp and never see him, but the very minute you would forget about him, he would bob up and scare the wits out of you."* (R. M. Harrison)

----------

Randy, Monica, and I conferred and we decided that Randy with his fast-working air scent Labrador, Josie, and Denise, as support, would venture down an old trail to try and reach the creek at the bottom of the north slope. After they headed out, we heard nothing more until they emerged from "below," several hours later. There were absolutely no reliable radio communications in this kind of wildness.

On the Josephine County SAR blog, Denise later described what transpired while they were out of radio communications.

"Ann mentions we "disappeared for hours," and so here is "the rest of the story:" We were asked to go down the trail to the creek, then proceed downstream to the point-last-seen (PLS), and come back up at the falls.

Randy and his black lab, Josie, proceeded me down an overgrown log road/trail. Our path ended, and off to the left a trail seemed to continue. We marked the location and down we went, steeper until I was holding onto branches to keep my footing on loose rock, sometimes sliding on my butt and stopping against a tree trunk, grabbing another branch and sidestepping down. We could hear the creek not far below so we "went for it."

The creek at this point was in a narrow sheer rock canyon, with huge log jams, boulders, curtains of moss covering everything and old growth timber towering above.

Randy turned to me. "What does this remind you of?"

"Dinosaurs should appear any moment," I replied.

"Yeah, like a T-rex." Randy said as Josie lapped her fill.

I thought of Jurassic Park, and wished I'd brought a camera. We edged along the creek, stepped on boulders, walked huge downed logs, crawled over logs, lifted Josie from logs, admired the falls and grottos, pressing downstream. At one point, I slipped and wet my feet in a pool, but it felt good.

Randy, leading the way, stopped short. He'd found a freshly opened MRE. We marked the place and he radioed command. Not far down, Josie barked an alert, but not her usual bark. She did this twice, at a rock and at the water. Randy and I felt strongly that scent was being carried down with the water. We found fresh cut maple saplings as well.

More saplings were cut where a small drainage connected with the creek. It seemed obvious that someone had gone up at this point, and we decided to follow. We checked our time; noon. For the next three hours, we climbed extremely steep slopes, again, I went from branch to branch of firs, maples, vine maples and even wild rhododendrons (making sure they were live ones!) to pull myself up. At times I had to scramble upwards on my hands and knees, kicking my toes into the duff, sliding down and trying to hold my position, clutching at ferns. The brush closed in around us and we pushed through it, crawled through and over it, stopping for a couple minutes here and there *to check our GPS for direction. We both agreed to keep moving, afraid we'd stiffen up if we rested too long.*

*Josie was fantastic, sticking close to Randy, but always checking the air with her nose. Perhaps halfway up, she became very interested, but at this point, we knew the conditions would never allow us to follow up on it. We were blessed to find plenty of water for Josie in the drainage, and kept refilling her bottles.*

*Finally, Randy gave a yell from his position above me. "Come on up here; you're not going to believe this!"*

*I gathered my strength, pushing up over a log, and clawed my way to reach him. Up over the edge, and we saw the end of the trail we had marked. We did it, we found our way. We sat on the edge with Josie and admired the view, and contemplated what we had just done. According to our GPS, we'd climbed 1300'. Randy shook my hand.*

*I wanted to shake Josie's paw, and wondered how she felt about our adventure. The dedication of our dogs is incredible. They trust us and even in the worst circumstances, seek to please us and do their job.*

*During the search this week in Ashland, I flanked for Ann and her dog, Connie. It was hot, the road steep, and Connie was tired. She sank down on her belly in some shade while Ann dosed her with water. After the break, we decided to head back. We'd gone several miles and hours already. Ann tugged the long line, but Connie stood firm, then resolutely turned and slowly continued uphill. Her nose told her this was the way. She would not give up.*

*My dog Cody greeted me when I returned home late after the Curry County search, vacuuming the scent off my legs, and gave me a look, lifting his eyebrow. He'd wanted to go with me, but his intermediate test isn't until later this fall. Gazing into his golden-brown eyes, I know he'll try his best to make me proud."*

----------

Beryl and I paired up with Monica and K9 Mara (a red coloured field-bred golden retriever) and Doug, who was also in the K9 Unit, but who's role today would be to provide support for both of us. Our first task was to scout along the rutted track to find someplace safe to begin our downward descent into the drainage in hopes of reaching the creek far below. While we found a place to begin our search, we never made it to the creek bottom. Instead, even after gingerly negotiating the terrain we only managed to descend a few hundred feet before being forced by vertical drop offs to traverse the slope back up toward our vehicles. It was beyond steep; we made excruciatingly slow progress only to be thwarted by sheer drops. The thick vegetation doing little to hold the loose soil in place; take one step, slide down two more. At one point, Monica and I got separated by one of the drop offs. Doug and I were forced to literally crawl up the side of the slope to the road. Monica successfully found an old trail and made her way back up. It was tough on the dogs. It was frustrating for us. We headed back to the command area.

We were given a second assignment. But, in order to even get to the assigned search area, we had to drive another 40 minutes along more hot and dusty gravel roads to the opposite side of the Sixes River drainage. We were asked to search as best we could the Little Dix Creek drainage. It was rumored there just might be an old road cut from the ridgetop at a place depicted on the map as the "Blue Jay Mine" that would lead us down to the creek to another place called "the falls" which was described to us as a 40-foot waterfall that fell into the canyon.

As we started our search efforts along the long-abandoned logging road numbered simply 392, Beryl flicked her head to the right into the direction of the wind. Doug exclaimed, "Did you see that?" I responded "Oh yes, let's mark this spot and take a compass bearing. It reads 65 degrees." Over my career, I was fortunate to have some of the best support personal as flankers, as they were called, and Doug was one of those. He was truly exceptional with a keen eye and he knew my dogs tells almost as well as I did. I was lucky to have him partnered with me during some of the most memorable and some of the most arduous searches of my career.

*K9 Beryl catching scent on the wind during training*

We trekked on, hacking and clawing our way through brush and small trees and climbing over larger fallen trees that laid across the old road which was now starting to resemble the forest from which it had been carved. Based on the number of elk droppings seen along the way, the big mammals were clearly major users of this track in the wilderness. We did reach the top of Little Dix Creek and we stood silent as we looked down. I did not like what I saw. Doug dropped down over the side for only about 50 feet just to get a "feel" for the area; it wasn't safe. As he made his way back up, he kicked rocks loose that we could hear crashing through the woods for what had to be several hundred feet. All of us are in good shape, very confident in our abilities, but this was just not safe and we weren't going down. Thwarted and frustrated yet again in our attempt to conduct some kind of meaningful search.

Not wanting to "give-up," we decided we would walk along the 393 road that appeared, on our rudimentary map, to circle the Little Dix Creek drainage. Maybe there was another, safer way, to descend. We turned around and headed back the way we came, all rather tired and frustrated, even the dogs. After climbing over yet another tree, a silent signal was exchanged between the "girls" and Mara decided to have a colourful discussion over the matter with Beryl. It shook me up a bit as Mara had the distinct advantage over "little B." Beryl was a little shaken up too but once the energy settled back down, she shook it off and quickly got back to work.

It was only a few steps later that we were all hit with another rush of warm air from across the drainage. Both dogs showed significant changes of behavior consistent with encountering scent on the wind - nose in the air, heads held up high and reaching to get a better sniff of what? of whom? Beryl chased the scent as it hit the steep cut bank along the road and tried to climb up the loose sandy soil to the top. What had they smelled? We recorded a bearing of 95 degrees.

We turned left onto the 393 road and continued along the ridge and around to the other side of the Little Dix drainage. At a wide landing along the road, we were met with a swirling gust of wind and both dogs immediately started dancing on their paws, racing from one end of the landing to the other trying to determine from which direction the scent was coming from. We took bearings on the wind direction but just like the dogs we were having trouble as one moment it appeared to come from the north and at the same time from the northwest but also from the northeast. We plotted the earlier bearing lines out about three-quarters of a mile, distances we estimated based on our best understanding of the terrain and wind before us and coupled with previous experiences we had from training and on searches with our canines. Everything seemed to be overlapping in the area where Little Dix and Rusty Creek dumped into the South Fork of the Sixes River. What we didn't realize at the time was that the wind reaching us from across the drainage was more direct in nature rather than the typical daily rise of warm air coming up from the drainage like we expected and assumed it to be. If we had considered that, we might have factored in that important piece of information; we were walking along the road at between 1,700 - 2,000 feet and Mr. Cox was holed up unbeknownst to us at approximately 1,600 feet.

I told Monica that I was going to continue a bit further along the road. Doug and I spied a very recently discarded candy wrapper lying in the middle of the dirt track. We called it in and we were informed the "family had walked the road the previous day." In hindsight, I wish they hadn't told us that as it influenced what we did next. At the next bend in the road the vegetation became crawl through thick again and the wind had died down in the terrain's shadow. We looked at each other and reluctantly turned around. We turned around too early. That decision, which you make in the moment and hope it's the right decision to make, still gnaws at me. I don't know if we would have found Mr. Cox that afternoon if we had continued along the road but if we had we would have saved him another night out in the wilds of the Sixes River. The 393 road dead-ended another 430 meters from where we turned around and William Cox was just over the ridge, another 225 meters away, weak and dehydrated in a dense steep patch of forest waiting and hoping for rescue.

As we walked back to our vehicles, Doug and I tossed around ideas of what those changes of behaviour could have meant. Had William aka "Jack" Cox tried to climb out using the old mining road to the Blue Jay Mine and took the wrong drainage? We couldn't even begin to go down the slope to find out. The dogs were tired, hot, and stressed. Beryl flushed a forest grouse, "I'm done," she said. We were all on no sleep and both physically and mentally exhausted. We drove the 40 minutes on the same dusty track back to base; there were so many thoughts swirling around in my tired head.

*Neither dog had performed their trained final response when hit with the rush of warm air. Was the scent too faint? Was it the scent of other searchers far far below? What had caused the behaviour change? Beryl didn't formally alert, but what I witnessed in her behaviour was so similar to my recent training experience in the Ochoco Mountains.*

It was late when we got back to base. Randy and K9 Josie and Denise had already checked out and were headed home. Monica and I debriefed directly with Sherriff John Bishop. We showed him our map with the locations marked of where the dogs had shown significant changes of behaviour and of the wind direction at the time. We even sketched it out again on a piece of note paper in an attempt to convey and explain our observations. I couldn't tell by the expression on his face if he was really grasping what we were trying to communicate or if he even thought it was noteworthy. Our clues were not something you could see or touch, they were born on training and trust between handler and canine. By the time we got back down the mountain the Pacific had all but swallowed the sun.

I heard on the news the next day that William Cox had been found alive. I wanted to learn more than what the news media was reporting on how he was found so I sent an email to Cathy, one of the Coos County canine handlers. She and I had worked together on the Clara search and I knew she had been working her dog on the day Mr. Cox was located. A couple of days later, I got a reply.

*Did not mean to take so long getting back to you. John and I were sent to the PLS. I had scented Lucky with a scent article and when we were down in the Rusty Creek drainage just up river from the PLS the guys that had driven us down on the ATV's were just ahead of us and they found his sleeping bag. Lucky insisted that he had scent up the cliff to our right as we were looking upriver. It was too steep to get up there but we called it in. As I understand it, the undersheriff took that info and put it together with info from the dogs the day before and decided to put the family into the area where he was found.*

*The family found a still warm campfire but no Mr. Cox. The dogs were being brought to the area and they said they could hear him but had not yet found him. As we were bringing in the dogs again, they found him about 100 yards from the campfire."*

Teamwork. SAR is not about one searcher or one dog, it's about a team of individuals working together toward a common goal, to put the pieces of the puzzle together, to bring someone home. One of the things that I learned very quickly during my SAR career was that there are so many clues out there - some of which are only carried on the wind – which just need to be expertly put together in order to find the missing or lost. When I started teaching Search Tactics and Land Navigation for our SAR Academy students, it was one of the points that I stressed. Pay attention, stay focused. Document those clues.

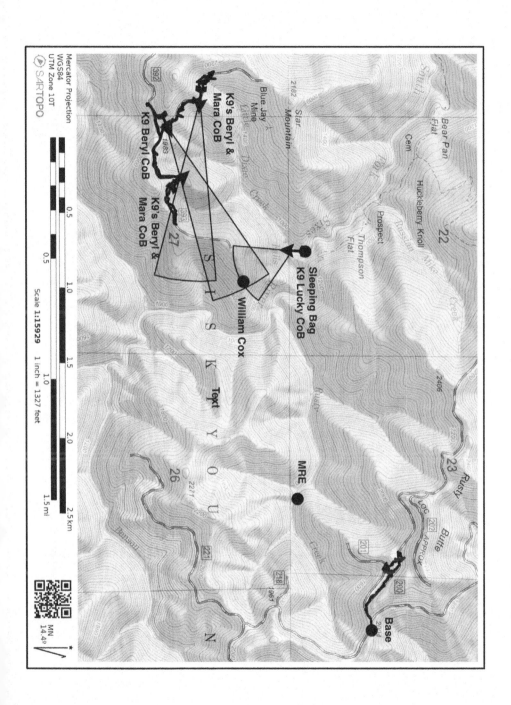

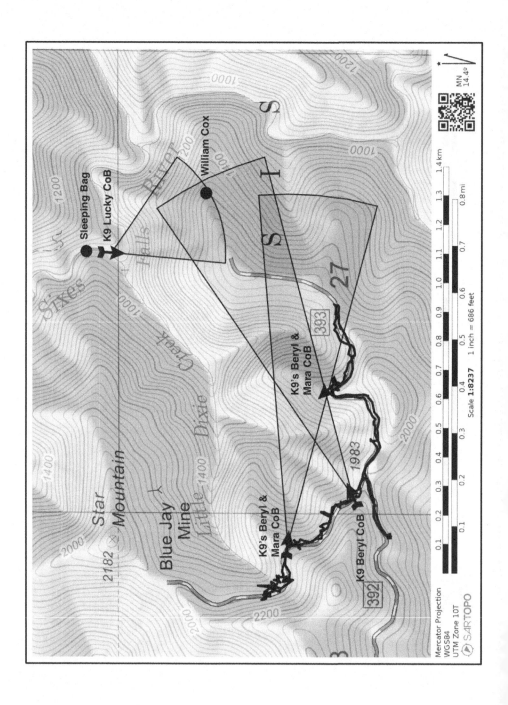

# The Conne Family Search

Some of the most challenging, physically exhausting, and mentally draining searchers took place along the Oregon coast. This search was no exception. On Sunday January 29th 2012, Belinda and Dan Conne and their son Michael plus Jessie, one of the family dogs, left their home to go mushroom gathering. Hedgehog or sweet tooth mushrooms to be exact; these mushrooms, when sold at market, would help this family make ends meet. According to press reporting, the family had only recently moved to Oregon for a fresh start. Life had been clearly rough for this family and I was hoping that any luck they still might have, hadn't run out.

*"Seven months earlier, they'd traveled from Duncan, Okla., to make a fresh start in Gold Beach, a small coastal community about 300 miles south of Portland. They were looking for a second chance. Daniel, 47, had done manual labor in Oklahoma, lifting heavy-duty truck parts and the work had wreaked havoc on his back. He'd gone under the knife three times. Doctors said there was nothing more they could do. He was on Social Security disability and got a small monthly check. Belinda, his 47-year-old wife, had worked as a bookkeeper in Oklahoma, but the only thing she could find in Gold Beach was a job as a motel maid. When winter tourism plummeted, however, the motel cut back on the staff. These days, she was lucky to get four hours a week. A few years earlier their son, Michael, had been in a jam with the law in Oklahoma. This could be a new beginning. At 25, he was looking for work in Gold Beach, but having no luck."* (Tom Hallman Jr., Oregon Live, February 6, 2012).

By the next day, when the family hadn't returned to their camp at Huntley Park, where they lived in a 25-foot trailer, neighbors reported the family missing to the Sherriff's Office. It wasn't until Wednesday February 1st, however, that their vehicle, a 2004 red Jeep Cherokee, was located. Curry County Sheriff Deputies had spent those two and half days scouring the myriad of backroads until eventually locating the vehicle on a muddy unremarkable dirt track designated simply as the 120 road. This obscure track headed south into the mountains from the main Gold Beach to Agnes Road. A hasty search was immediately conducted and about 1/4 mile to the south of the vehicle several articles of clothing were found and some totes to carry mushrooms, but no other sign of the family. Due to the extreme rugged terrain, a CORSAR callout was done immediately, on that Wednesday evening.

Thursday morning started early. We departed our SAR barn at 0500 for the 140-mile drive to the command area, set up at Quosatana Creek Campground. Our early arrival allowed the canine teams to get a head start before the ground teams were deployed. In the back of my little red Subaru Forester were K9's Beryl and Winston. Winston was half-brother to Beryl and was two years her senior. He had certified in mantrailing about a year and a half earlier, in October of 2010, and already had one successful find to his name. He was teaching me that mantrailing dogs could also pick-up air scent from long distances. Getting SAR Managers to believe what our dogs were communicating to us was turning out to be the difficult part. Two other canine teams from Josephine County also made the trek over, Monica and K9 Mara and Denise with her newly certified golden retriever, K9 Cody. Eight ground searchers and three designated flankers rounded out the Josephine County contingent.

Our team that day, designated Team 1, consisted of myself with K9 Winston, Joe from Josephine County, and then out of an abundance of caution I suspect, two additional flankers both of whom had been in the field the previous day. There was John, from Coos County who was training a canine and then Chris who was the son of John Bishop, the Curry County Sheriff. I wasn't really comfortable having so many people tagging along; it can be distracting and I had no idea of their physical fitness. Winston might not be a big guy, but he had a big heart and surprised many with his agility despite his 40 stocky pounds on his 15-inch-high body frame. That low center of gravity had its advantages. We were the first trailing dog team on site, so our assignment was to try and find a trail leading to the missing or perhaps get at least a solid direction of travel. It was now day five that this family had been out in the woods, finding a trail was going to be tough but maybe we would find other clues.

My first question before we headed out from command was "is my vehicle suitable for the spur road?" Not such a crazy question, even for a Subaru, as my little red car had been on some very rough roads trying to navigate us to a last-known-point (LKP). Well, it was muddy but we

made it. On a positive note, after several days of wet weather, the front had cleared and we were left with clear hazy skies and cool temperatures. As we started our search efforts that morning at 0930, I noted that we still had downslope winds. It

*K9 Winston negotiating a typical deployment environment* had been quite cool that morning and the slopes faced north as they tumbled down toward the Rogue River. The mountainous terrain along the river would also undoubtedly cause very localized air movements and probably even areas of stagnant or pooling air, especially in the hollows and depressions and areas containing the thickest vegetation. While immediately around the vehicle the area was open and meadow like, the rest of the area was wilderness with all that that envisions. Moderate to steep drainages, a swift flowing creek swollen with all the recent heavy rains, vegetation described as typical coastal rainforest with extremely thick undergrowth of huckleberry, rhododendrons, vine maple, fern, and moderate downfall.

I collected a scent article using a 2 x 2 gauze pad to transfer the scent of the missing from a fold in the back of the passenger side seat of the jeep to the gauze pad which was then sealed in a Ziploc bag. I chose this seat rather than using the driver's seat on the assumption that Law Enforcement had looked around in the vehicle for any clues that would help them in their investigation and this often translates into the driver's side of the vehicle being disturbed the most.

I presented the scent article to K9 Winnie, who took a good sniff and starting leading us south along a dirt track but only for a short-ways; he then turned toward a drainage draped in thick green vegetation immediately to the west and then circled us back to the jeep. We had made a circle, not uncommon as he sorted through a myriad of scents and odors and tried to make olfactory sense of his surroundings. Within that circle, my support eyed a cigarette pack and a near empty Gatorade bottle about 30 feet from the vehicle that most likely belonged to the missing family. K9 Winnie, with more certainty now, circled the vehicle one more time and then headed back toward the drainage and started heading with purpose southward; he existed the drainage into a meadow and continued south, his pace increasing.

It's funny how certain moments just stick in your memories and what happened next is one of them. As we crested a small rise in the meadow we were met with a strong downslope wind (noted at the time as bearing 222 degrees) and Winston raised his head and lifted his nose high into the air. I had seen this before. I asked Joe to mark this location on his GPS (10T 397477E 4704458N) and I did the same as Winston set his nose into the wind and leaned into his harness.

The meadow transitioned back to forest and then we were on a dirt track; Winston leading us directly to the clothing and mushroom buckets, clues discovered the previous day by a hasty team. Winston kept heading south until everything changed; Winnie encountered a scent pool or was it a proximity alert? We instinctively hit mark on our GPS (10T 397036E 4703827N) units as every fiber in Winston's short stocky strong body screamed "I've got them!"

In his excitement, he became a bit manic pulling me down into a deep depression to our left. It was steep but Joe followed. The forest floor here was mostly clear of heavy vegetation, but the trees towered above us, leaving an impression of being inside a huge cathedral. My other two support personal followed but I noticed they were becoming hesitant in their movements. Winston ran back up toward the track and then turned back around and dove back down the slope. By about the third loop down into the "hole," I noticed John and Chris remained up on the track and had stopped following. When Winston broke through the scent pool and started further southward, John mentioned his knee was acting up and Chris wasn't looking like he was enjoying himself. I suggested they both head back together to the LKP and they could probably hitch a ride back to command. To be honest, I was kind of glad to see them go.

K9 Winston proceeded south until the track we were on came to an abrupt end (10T 396860E 4703828N, point marked as #774). That same downslope wind was present, we took a bearing, our compass' read 242 degrees. As we stood at the end of the track Winston's head raised catching scent on the wind, Joe and I just looked with awe at the magnitude and beauty of the scene laid before us: a massive sea of thick green vegetation lining a steep bowl-shaped drainage that reached up toward an unseen ridge far above. Small rays of sunlight breaking through the tree canopy lighting the scene in spectacular fashion as if we were on the set of major motion picture, the classic movie Jurassic Park came to mind. Our forward progress was abruptly halted. Winnie knew, but we could not continue. From my search report:

At this point we started retracing our path and K9 Win again showed a significant change of behaviour at 10T 397036E 4703827N. As we worked back north along the dirt track, K9 Winnie stopped twice, raised his head to the west and again indicated strong air scent. We then continued north back toward the subject's vehicle when K9 Win encountered one more pocket of scent (point #775; 10T 397284E 4704017N) in the draw to the east; however, he showed no interest in continuing east. This change of behavior was in a direct line and consistent with his other indications.

K9's behaviour was consistent with being in scent and on task from LKP to 10T 396860E 4703828N. We could not proceed further south due to terrain restriction. K9 also showed interest in trying to move westward as well as south.

By the time we returned to my little red Subaru, it was two in the afternoon. We drove back to base to report our findings.

**Suggestions for Further Search Efforts:** Suggest the area and the draw to the west (and south) of where the clothing and mushroom buckets be searched. Also suggest searching the entire drainage from subject's vehicle southward.

All of these years later and after reading my official report, I regret not having been more detailed in my suggestions for further search efforts. I do recall, however, in my verbal debriefing clearly pointing at the map to the drainage south of our furthest point, where the track had ended at the steep impenetrable wall of green. All of our GPS points where Winston had demonstrated clear changes of behaviour were shared with command. I recall the next day mentioning "to the south" several times to command while I waited for my next assignment and helped with some debriefs. When I read the official after-action report of the search it made no mention of any of the scent clues Winston provided. It wasn't the lack of recognition that bothered me, it was that all of the canine's scent clues (several other K9 teams had reported back with scent clues as well) had been so easily dismissed that I found so disheartening and frustrating as this is exactly the type of information that potentially could save a life someday.

By the end of Thursday, a few more possible physical clues were located but the Conne family was still missing. Most of the Josephine County searchers opted to spend the night at a local hotel in the seaside town of Gold Beach so we would be fresh for Day 2. Taking a shower, changing into clean clothes, and sharing a pizza in the parking lot, all good memories. And as searchers tend to do, we talked about the search, what we did, what we should have done if we could have, what we think happened to the family, all sorts of theories and conjecture. The next day we would all try to do our best yet again.

Search assignments were handed out the next day but from my report I did not get an assignment until the afternoon. I'm not clear after all these years why that was the case or exactly what I did all those hours waiting to go out again. I vaguely recall helping with debriefs in the command trailer and probably suggesting, to the point of being a bit of a nuisance, that teams be sent further south into the drainage.

It was 1230 in the afternoon when we received our next assignment. This time for K9 Beryl. Four pails of mushrooms had just been located by a ground search team at 10T 0396908E 4704349N. Our assignment was to search around this location and toward the south. I was lucky to have Joe back flanking but also Ron, another Josephine County searcher who would flank numerous times for me over the years. We were now Team 10. Back up the now very rutted road to the LKP. It was now 1341 hours. It took us another 20 minutes of fast hiking to get to our assigned area and we commenced our search at two o'clock in the afternoon on a February day. Sunset was scheduled for 1720, leaving us only a few hours of daylight.

With the limited daylight we had available, my search plan was to start Beryl about 50 feet north of the mushroom buckets found on the dirt track where the day before we noted a small path heading west from here. This would be a logical way to proceed to the field cache just discovered. As we headed west, Beryl showed a slight change of behavior at 10T 397090E 4704324N below a 15-20 feet cliff. Her head was up and looking south, and she tried to climb the cliff bank. I knew a ground team had been in the area but I still made sure to mark my GPS with this information. We discovered a way up and over the rocky cliff bank and came upon an old barely discernable skid road that led us directly to the field cache. While this road was depicted on our maps, even while standing on it, it was barely visible to the eye. It had long ago been abandoned back to the coastal forest. From the buckets we spiraled out and crossed the drainage above a waterfall and climbed upward until we reached a very well-maintained gravel road. Other than maybe some slight interest as we crossed over the drainage, Beryl was unimpressed with this area. I decided to head back to the mushroom cache via the old skid road that we had noted earlier and then continue along this overgrown route, which was heading south, and see where it led us.

As we proceeded along the track, all of a sudden at 10T 397063E 4704221N, K9 Beryl showed a significant change of behavior; so significant that I expected her to perform her jump alert. Wind direction was downslope from the south on a bearing of approximately 213 degrees.

What does *"Beryl showed a significant change of behaviour"* mean anyway. Well, I had seen this now many times, during previous searches and during trainings. I knew what it meant. The look in her eyes, the head carriage, the animation in her step. It meant she had a nose full of scent and just like Winston the day before "she had them." Beryl drove ahead into the brush and like a rabbit she navigated through the twisted branches with ease. We were on our hands and knees crawling, getting tangled, inching forward and when we couldn't crawl, we simply walked over the top of the mangled vegetation. The old road was getting harder and harder to follow now. It was getting late and we were requested to return to "base." "No, she had scent!" my head screamed to no one but myself. As a group, we decided we hadn't heard the radio transmission and kept following as best we could but at-some-point we realized it was time to return. I knew we could still be a considerable distance from the lost and it was getting late. Command was requesting again for everyone to return-to-base.

We pulled out our compasses and in conjunction with our GPS units used them both together in order to find the main dirt track that would lead us north and back to my car. That "road" was only 200 feet away but navigating to it was still quite a challenge. When we did finally reach the track, we stood above a very steep cutbank. We headed south, paralleling the track looking for a safe place to descend which we eventually found.

As each of us carefully descended the cutbank, Beryl made one last ditch effort to get me to follow. She raced back into the brush, turned around and looked directly into my eyes and pleaded with me in a silent language shared between partners: "Please, please follow me, I know the way, it's this way!" I slipped from her view down the cutbank and a moment later she appeared and reluctantly followed me down. That pleading look in her eyes has haunted me for years, it still haunts me. Why hadn't I just followed?

We hustled as quickly as we could back to my vehicle, threw our gear in and rushed down the muddy road. It was now 1720. Sunset. Thump. What was that? I kept driving until we reached the main highway, the thumping continued and I was forced to stop. Joe and Ron peered under my car and pried loose a six-foot branch that had punctured clear through the plastic skid plate.

As we drove into the Quosatana Campground, it was clear that search efforts for the day were mostly done. Most of the parking lot was empty, only a few vehicles and the large motorhome serving as the command post remained. We were, in fact, the last team in from the field. I literally ran into the command post with my "clue." I was being debriefed while command was in the process of closing shop. Was anyone listening? The debriefer took my information but the SAR Managers were all leaving and heading out to make search plans for the next day. I found Sara, Josephine County's SAR Coordinator, and tried to explain what Beryl had so clearly told me. She nodded. And base emptied. A new Incident Command Team was taking over the search for the next day, for Operational Period 4. From my official search report:

**Suggestions for Further Search Efforts:** Suggest the area in and around where Beryl showed the significant change of behavior be thoroughly searched; proceed outward and to the south up the draw. I also believe the trail we found was the one probably used by the family as the only logical way into where the mushroom bucket cache was discovered. As happened to us, it was easy to get turned around as the skid road evaporated into dense huckleberry.

Since we hadn't found the subjects, it felt like no one was really listening or understanding what I was saying. This was day two and both of my dogs had communicated to me the same thing, to the south up the drainage! Again, in reading the after-action review of the search, I have no sense if their scent clues were used to help shape the search efforts the following day. When looking at the physical clues and the GPS tracks showing where ground and canine teams had already searched, to the south and up the drainage was the next logical direction to search. Maybe the scent information wasn't relevant. But, the canine scent clues were valuable pieces of information and yet it seemed very few were willing to accept the concept of the "long-distant alert."

----------

*Aerial view of where the family was found*

The Conne family and their dog were located on Saturday February 4th at 1114 am by John Rachor, well-known pilot who helped on many SAR missions. He had been the pilot who located Kati Kim and her two daughters stranded in the snow six years earlier. He also would locate Steven Ivy during one of Tollie's last searches almost six years later (see the *Puck Lake* story). The Conne family was found up the drainage to the south.

They recounted to the media what had happened while they waited and prayed to be rescued.

*"A powerful rainstorm, the towering old growth trees and always looking at the ground to find mushrooms made the family lose their bearings. By nightfall, they were lost. Daniel Conne knew the rules: Stay put.*

*But the cellphone didn't have a signal and finally its battery died.*

*They'd each eaten a peanut butter sandwich before leaving home. That would have to hold until morning. They fashioned a rustic, lean-to out of scavenged wood, but it collapsed and in the soaking rain no one slept.*

*Sunrise was no better. They rain didn't let up. They weren't sure what direction to turn. Hungry and thirsty, they fought panic. In the distance, they heard a creek and set out to find water. But they had to climb down a long, steep hillside that played havoc with Daniel Conne's back. In his pocket, he had a couple plastic sandwich bags he used to keep toilet tissue dry. He threw away the paper and gave the bags to his son, who walked to the creek, filled the bags and carried them back.*

*Replenished, they knew they had to get back up the hill and find a way out of the woods. But as night fell again, they knew they were in trouble.*

*Michael Conne found a massive old-growth tree that had fallen and was rotting from the inside. He used a knife to carve out the middle, creating a place where the family and dog could rest.*

*The days and nights passed.*

*The family tried hitting stones together, hoping to catch some tinder on fire, but the effort made only sparks. Each day, Michael made the long, treacherous climb down the hill to the creek to fill the sandwich bags and carry them up the hill to the log they now called home.*

*On Tuesday, he fell into the water. Before long, he was suffering from hypothermia and couldn't move. His mother took over water duty. Days later, she was so weak she had to get help from her husband, even though he could hardly walk. They helped each other up and down the hill. Then Daniel Conne could no longer walk. His wife made the water run alone.*

*By now they'd been in the woods for five days.*

*Daniel Conne tried eating a mushroom, but couldn't stand the taste. His wife and son passed. They thought about eating ants. And, if it came to it, killing Jessie for the meat. The dog was loyal, staying close to the family and snuggling next to them as they fought to stay warm."*

----------

As I often did after a search was completed, I studied what my dogs and I had done, or hadn't done, and poured over the maps and satellite imagery now so easily available on the internet. What I noticed when reviewing older satellite imagery (circa 1994) was a logging road scar that led southwestward and up the drainage from the mushroom cache found on Friday, the day I deployed Beryl. This track was not denoted on any of the search maps and as old roads do, they fade away as the forest reclaims her land. This was the old road that we attempted to follow when Beryl told us "this way." The maps show it reconnecting to the more established track but it actually continues southwest. The Conne family was near this now old road when they were located; it's

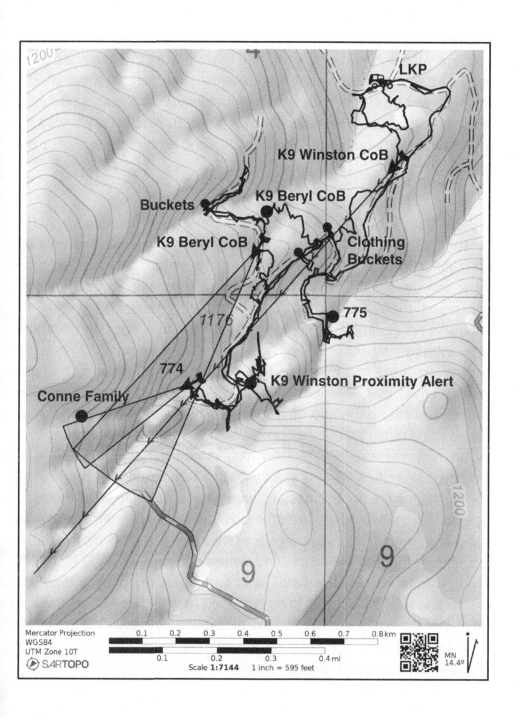

possible they either knowingly or unknowingly followed it up the drainage. Winston had only been 350 meters from the family when we stood at the end of that small track overlooking the vast impenetrable drainage and he clearly indicated "up that way." Beryl was a bit further down the drainage, 730 meters (or 2,400 feet), when she showed me through her body language and her pleading eyes, that she also had the family's scent.

----------

Beryl first certified in wilderness human remains detection (HRD) in the summer of 2010. She certified every two years after that until her last certification in 2016. As time went on, it seemed that more and more of my searches with Beryl were HRD searches and, in fact, her logs reflect just that. I more often than not was asked to deploy my mantrailing dogs and Beryl waited in the vehicle for assignments that came infrequently. At Unit trainings, she always seemed to be last in the training cue. I had two dogs to run most of the time and I had also become the Unit Leader in early 2009 which meant greater responsibilities; hence she often got the short-shrift at trainings. Plus, she was just getting older, her body wasn't as agile as it once was and her hearing was starting to fade which limited her ability to deploy on large area searches. That horse injury seemed to plague us more and more as time wore on; at times she would hesitate when I cued "search" especially in those steep treacherous environments we were often asked to search in. Her message was becoming clear to me, "It hurts," she said. In the late spring of 2012, when she 8 years old, I did a little trailing with her but by this time Tollie had joined my pack and he was just starting his trailing training so I decided to unclip Beryl from the long line. Although her logs show she still did air scent problems, her primary focus became HRD. We did some training for water recovery and attended a couple of water seminars over the years as well but she never certified in the discipline. She loved to work from the boat though or from along the shore and we were asked to assist on a few water recoveries. I think we both enjoyed the challenge of trying to pinpoint

and strategize where a body could be located based on where the scent was emerging from the water. Water search and recovery efforts in Josephine County focused along two major river systems, the Rogue and Illinois Rivers. Both of these rivers have been designated Wild and Scenic along a great portion of their westward journey to the ocean and boast some excellent fishing and other recreational opportunities. They are also cold rivers and unforgiving if you make a mistake on their waters.

What follows are two of the most memorable HRD searches that Beryl and I were involved in. The first spanned two seasons, 2011 and 2012, and the second search lasted just two days in 2014. Both of these searches left a lasting impression on me. The first because the mystery was never solved, the second because of the scope of the search, and both because of the emotions involved.

# A Sacred Place

It was 2006 and little boy named Sammy went missing on a crisp fall Saturday afternoon at Crater Lake National Park while with his father touring the park. They stopped at Cleetwood Cove to take in the breathtaking scenery and when it was time to get back into the car, Sammy reportedly raced across Rim Road up the ash covered embankment into the dark woods beyond and was never seen again. He was only eight years old and had Asperger's syndrome which falls along the higher functioning end of the autism spectrum. I waited by the phone, checked my pager several times a day, anticipating that Josephine County would be called to come to the Park and assist in the search. Janet called and we wondered why the call hadn't come. She made several phone calls and finally by Wednesday afternoon she called me back and said we could go. She was to bring K9 Angie, her bloodhound, and she wanted me and Mike, a very experienced Josephine County searcher, to assist.

*Mike, Myself, and K9 Angie*
*Crater Lake National Park*

We spent two days following Angie through the deep woods and across the pumice soils as she tried to connect "scent dots" together. She worked hard, focused on her task seemingly oblivious to both the terrain and the ever-changing weather conditions. The first day snow blanketed the ground and the air felt like winter while the second day we were under a blazing Indian summer sky. There were times when we all felt she was on Sammy's trail. On day two a helicopter followed us as Angie followed scent across the pumice soils. In my support position I got to practice some of my navigation skills but I think our extraction the first day had more than a little luck involved. I plotted us a direct line through an area called Mazama Rocks – a mass of jumbled volcanic rocks with false paths, dead end rock canyons, and steep and dangerous cliffs – and by some miracle my plan worked. We spent the night at the Diamond Lake Resort and ate granola bars and leftover peanut butter sandwiches from the days sack lunch and then dived into the stash of peanut butter sandwiches Janet brought from home. I ate more peanut butter sandwiches and granola in those two days than I ever had in my life. After two full days of searching and no sign of Sammy we headed home as the search officially ended. It had only been a week. The three of us were so tired as Mike maneuvered the old SAR rig back down the mountain that we became giddy; someone made a silly joke about what I have no recollection but it just might have had something to do with peanut butter sandwiches and we laughed until our stomachs hurt. Inside we were actually all so sad.

----------

I returned to Crater Lake to search for Sammy at every opportunity. Sometimes only as a ground searcher, but in 2011 and again in 2012 as a canine handler. Plans for follow on canine searches were planned but never materialized due to weather and circumstance. My last search experience for Sammy came nine years after the first, in 2015, as a ground searcher. None of the searches ever uncovered any physical clues of what had happened to Sammy.

That first canine search with Beryl came in 2011 and was possibly one of my best SAR experiences, certainly one of the most memorable. It was a search filled with passion, but also filled with friendship, good food, and some serious laughs. It was mostly a Josephine County affair; a National Park search organizer and a forensic expert from the Oregon State Medical Examiner's Office, Human Identification Program also took part but they had their own search plans for the weekend. We were also joined by another canine handler from Idaho and her black Labrador, however, she opted to stay in a local hotel.

If you've ever been down State Highway 138 there is a long straight stretch of road that runs downhill from Crater Lake National Park's north entrance until it ends at Highway 97, known as the Diamond Lake Junction. About 4 miles from that "T" intersection a dirt road, FSR 70 turns south at a 90-degree angle. There is a sign at the turn which reads Desert Creek Research Natural Area; this research area is noted for its excellent representation of unlogged and ungrazed ponderosa and lodgepole pine with antelope bitterbrush steppe. I can attest to the magnificent ponderosa pines in this area. It was this dusty wash boarded road we turned down on a Friday afternoon. Sara, our SAR Coordinator, was bringing our County's "new" command rig – a repurposed motorhome. As she drove down the last section of the bumpy road, she passed under some trees that were not quite as tall as the top of the motor home, a branch or two sacrificed for the cause. The command vehicle was also going to serve as home-away-from-home for the girls who would bunk in the toy hauler portion of the rig. Denise, with her horse trailer hauling expertise, pulled the porta-potty trailer behind one of the old SAR Chevy Suburban's. Lynda, Doug, myself and Beryl, rode with Denise rather than bring our personal vehicles. Monica drove her personal vehicle with K9 Mara; Brian drove his vehicle and came to set up vital communications; Ron hauled his little pop-up camper for he and Doug to share while Brian was going to brave the frigid night in a tent. At least the wind wasn't blowing as he set it up! One of my fondest and funniest memories of Brian was at a regional training hosted by Jackson County in 2006 at Johnson Prairie on the Jackson-Klamath border. The wind was blowing fiercely and Brian had forgotten to stake his tent down resulting in a hilarious "Fenton" moment of Brian chasing his cartwheeling tent across the dusty camping area. Brian is rather a heavy-set man and the tent almost won. Beryl and I slept in a toy hauler during that training weekend as well which was only slightly warmer than a tent. I remember Beryl snuggling with me in my sleeping bag and getting up in the night to give Sue, a fixture in SAR for so many years as an "everything women," puppy kisses.

By the time the morning broke it was freezing. Clear nights on the east side of the Cascades mean bitter cold. Ron was trying to fire-up the portable grill to cook a warm breakfast for everyone but the gas lines were frozen solid. Not sure how he solved the dilemma but we did get hot coffee and pancakes that morning, that much I remember. We were divided into two search teams. Monica & K9 Mara, Denise, and Ron were Team Sierra and K9 Beryl and I, Doug, and Lynda designated Team November.

Our assignment that day was to search an area of some 500 acres for human remains or articles that were now five years old. The search area followed the mostly flat dry Desert Creek and led west until the terrain rose into undulating hills surrounding a point on a map labeled

MT5662. Dry grasses, small junipers and manzanita, covered the ash soils along Desert Creek with large ponderosa pine bordering the creek's banks. As the elevation rose, the hills became forested and the forest floor was a thick layer of sharp pine needles and pine cones. We were lucky in that our assigned area only had moderate levels of downfall. There was also an old road cut running north to south and dividing the hills from the flat plain.

*K9 Beryl searching along Desert Creek, Crater Lake National Park*

Nothing significant happened that day. Teams got a late start, 1100 hours and by about 1500 hours we had decided to return to base as Beryl's pads were hurting her from all the abrasive pumice and the thick pine duff poking at her feet. As we headed back, we searched through the woods on the north side of Desert Creek. We finally arrived back at command at 1730 hours. We were tired and dusty. Beryl rested in her crate in the back of the RV and got a special supper of duck with her kibble. We had a big spaghetti feed with sourdough garlic bread and it all tasted divine. We downloaded search tracks and talked about the day and planned for an earlier start the next day.

We had barely scrapped the surface of our search area the day before, so today we tasked ourselves with trying to cover more of the western section, an area of roughly 300 acres.

As we entered our search area, Beryl exhibited a change of behaviour and then promptly gave me her trained air scent indication, jumping hard and hitting my legs with her paws. It was an air scent alert and not her trained final response for human remains but we still searched around the pile of downed logs that had caught her initial interest. Later that evening we learned that our search organizer and the forensic scientist had been in this exact area the day prior. About midpoint through this second day, we were asked to redirect to a point about a mile away where one of the other canines had displayed interest, significant enough for the handler to call it in. We took a look at our maps and noticed an old road cut; we exchanged smiles and

*The downfall encountered on the old road cut.  Doug looking after Beryl during a rest break*

expressed "how fortunate" we were as we could now make excellent time using the road rather than having to go cross country through the heavy downfall. We didn't get very far and only made it about half the distance to our destination before we were forced to turn around due to the thickest downfall I had ever seen and small lodgepole pines so tightly spaced that walking in any direction was near impossible. Poor Beryl was having a tough time negotiating the terrain. She had to jump over and over and over and over. Her body was tired. We stopped to take a break and she fell asleep in the water dish that Doug always carried for her. It was time to head back to command and to head home.

We had done a fair amount organizing for the trip home before we started our search efforts and Sara had been cleaning and getting the motorhome ready to roll as soon as we returned from the field. Denise was pulling the porta-potty trailer on the return trip as well and Lynda, Doug, myself and Beryl rounded out the cab crew. We were talking all about the search efforts and the fun we had had as a group. We were tired but had that giddy post search adrenaline rush still going. Some jokes were made, it was a fun time bonding with friends. Then somewhere around Union Creek, Monica pulls up alongside us in her vehicle, looks over and starts making these weird gestures at us. "What is she doing?" Known to drive a little fast and hurried, we kind of all just looked at each other with odd looks and laughed. Then one of us turned around and noticed sparks behind us lighting up the darkening forest. Then we notice there was toilet paper streaming out along the road behind us as well. Maybe we should pull over? We pull over to discover the right rear tire on the trailer was flat as one of Ron's pancakes! How we hadn't noticed, I have no idea. How Denise hadn't noticed, I have no idea. I suspect it had something to do with the less than stellar handling of the old vehicle she was driving in the first place. For some reason we all thought this was the funniest thing to happen ever, sparks that could have started a forest fire – it was, after all, late September – or maybe it was the overfilled porta-potty with the toilet paper streamers. There really was no other option but to laugh. Ron stopped and between he and Doug's dry sense of humor we were still laughing hysterically when Monica and Sara turned up. Did we have a vehicle jack? Uh, no. More laughter. There was one in the motorhome which was parked a few miles down the road at a little snow park so that was retrieved for us since using the logs technique, like they do in the movies, just wasn't going to work. Did we have a spare? Sort of, it wasn't in the best shape

but we did have one. While Ron worked to get us sorted, the rest of us mostly stood around and found something funny to laugh about. Adrenaline, exhaustion, it does bring out the giggles. Tyre fixed and we were on our way. As we pulled into the SAR compound in Merlin, the spare went flat.

*Ron fixing the flat while the rest of us mostly watch and laugh*

----------

In 2012, a larger group of canine handlers and other searchers met to try and bring Sammy home. This is that story.

The Klamath tribes refer to Crater Lake as "giiwas" or a scared place; a place where spirits and particular powers inhabit the volcanic terrain.

*"Here their medicine-men still come, as they always came in the olden time, to study spiritual wisdom and learn the secrets of life from the Great Spirit. In the solitude of these wilds they fasted and did penance; to the shores of the wierd [sic] lake they ventured with great danger, to listen to the winds that came from no one knew where--borne there to roam the pent-up waters and*

*bear the mysterious whispers of unseen beings, whose presence they doubted not, and whose words they longed to understand. They watched the shifting shadows of night and day; the hues of sun-light, moon-light, and star-light; saw white sails glisten on the moon-lit waters; caught the sheen of noiseless paddles, as they lifted voiceless spray, and having become inspired with the supernal, they bore back to their tribes charmed lives and souls fenced in with mystery."* (Klamath Land, Overland Monthly, VII, n.6, December 1873, p.553)

I think we all felt this power, the mystery of this place while searching for any sign of Sammy, a young boy of eight who wandered off and went missing six years ago this month. This was my fourth time up to the lake. I participated during the initial search, then three-years later, and then the last two years with my canine partner, Beryl. Many of the searchers this past weekend had been looking for as long and some much longer than I. It's an investment not only of time but of emotion. Every search leaves an impression on the soul, like footprints in the sand some of which are washed away while other remain, just out of reach from the tides.

So, we gathered. There were four California Rescue Dog Association dog handlers and their canines (two Labrador's, one golden retriever, and one border collie) and two dog teams from Josephine County (another golden retriever and a Sussex spaniel). Support personnel from Josephine, Klamath, Jackson, and Lane counties rounded out the search compliment. The search was managed and organized in coordination with National Park Service. Sammy's mother, aunt, and step-father were also in attendance, at peace but hopeful.

Our first briefing was Friday night at 2000 hours. It was an orderly and professional affair. The search areas were primarily to the east of the point-last-seen (PLS); planners had been reviewing old search reports (including canine data obtained from previous years efforts), studying the flow of the landscape, and likely paths of travel. All this data was then used to build search areas for the canine teams. After the briefing and receiving the next day's assignments, we all went back to our respective park service cabins, one for the boys and one for the girls (gotta love government regulations), and started entering the coordinates of our search areas into our GPS systems. We checked gear and then packed and repacked gear, the scene not unlike a group of soldiers readying for a special op. The fact that our search areas, Alpha through Oscar, were designated by the military alphabet added to the illusion. I'm not sure anyone really slept well that night and even though most alarms were set for 0500, the cabin started to come alive much earlier.

It was cold and dark at 0600 when we met to coordinate transportation out to our designated search areas. Josephine County's K9 Mara and K9 Beryl were assigned areas toward the very far eastern side of the park. We drove in two vehicles down from Rim Drive toward the ponderosa and lodgepole pine forests, to areas where drainages

*An old road cut in Area "F"*

ran silent and dry, and the soils were mostly layers of pumice and ash deposited during the last volcanic eruption, some 7,700 years ago. The temperature kept dropping, 19 degrees. Burr. Beryl was oblivious and enjoyed her ride sitting on my lap in the back of the vehicle while stealing kisses from Denise and Doug. Speaking of stealing, at some point during the drive, the brown beast managed to eat most of a banana, peel and all, that I had grabbed and stuffed in my cargo pants pocket on the way out the door. I have no idea how she did this without me noticing, but she did. My sneaky cheeky monkey.

Area Foxtrot was our assignment. This 500-acre parcel of land held within it a creek, dry as a bone this time of year, pumice soils, spindly lodgepole pines, copious downfall, magnificent old-growth ponderosa pine, and thick patches of manzanita on the higher slopes. Beautiful, wild, and silent. We searched all day, following natural paths and letting the terrain pull us where it may. Nothing. Dogs in other sectors were showing "changes of behaviour" and, in a couple of instances, giving their handler a trained alert. We eliminated an area by coming up empty; not very exciting but very important information to report.

Debriefs completed by 1900 hours, it was time for a quick shower and food! Josephine County hosted a spaghetti feed in the girl's cabin and nothing taste better after a long day of work but pasta for this Italian girl. Sammy's mom stopped by and we all talked about our  day and what was in store for Sunday. Another early start although this time alarms were needed to waken the tired crews at 0500. Everyone seemed to move just a tad bit slower than the day before, but with the same sense of purpose of mission. Not surprising as virtually all teams had spent eight hours in the field, travelling up to ten miles through, at times, extremely tough terrain at elevations ranging from 5,500 to 7,000 feet.

*K9 Beryl working the basalt tongue in Area Kilo*

On day two we were assigned Area Kilo. Instead of the overwhelmingly large search areas of the day before, today's areas were smaller, each about 40 acres or so, and were designed for focused thorough searching. Area Kilo was one of the furthest out from the PLS, over two miles from Cleetwood Cove. We hiked for roughly two hours to reach our area, the end of one of the ancient basalt flows, where the lines on the map can best be described, as we jokingly say, as "little-bitty lines really close together." Thankfully, there was a cut down through the basalt into the search area, the center of which was dusty and made well-trodden by years and years of elk, deer, bear, and other assorted animals. Downfall choked narrow sections while rock out-cropping's and sheer cliffs lined the side walls. Beryl was interested here and searched the area but couldn't seem to put her nose on it. Her behaviour was markedly changed and we hit the mark button on the GPS recording the location and made notes on her behaviour. We rested at the bottom of the draw and then searched southwest along the rocky base of "the basalt tongue," Beryl continuing to check around the rocks and in the thick piles of discarded and eaten pine cones and wherever a tree was torn up by bears.

It was about this time that an urgent voice was heard over the radio, "Did anyone have any hydrogen peroxide?" A handler's dog had just ingested an unknown type of white mushroom. I made a mental note to myself to start carrying hydrogen peroxide for just such emergencies as it can be used to induce vomiting and help rid the system of toxins. Her team began a hurried and nervous trek back to base while a team inserted to assist; thankfully, her dog was okay and the unknown mushroom not poisonous.

We were about out of time as Incident Command requested teams be out of the field by 1400hrs. We headed back up through another area of "little-bitty lines really close together" and plotted a route back to Cleetwood Cove. It's all uphill, roughly a 1000-foot climb up the caldera slope through a heavy mantle of conifer – pines, firs, and mountain hemlocks growing

*Lucky and Doug documenting our search efforts*

in pure bodies or mingled together. Beryl was starting to show the first signs of fatigue and I could tell that her feet were getting sore after miles and miles of walking through pumice and pine-cone duff several inches to feet thick. Then as we crested a small hill along another well-worn game path, she dropped into a formal down which is part of her trained final response. What? This wasn't the down of a tired fatigued dog; it was a perfect obedience down and she was alert and animated. She hadn't displayed all her normal body language indicators that would communicate to me that she was in odor of human remains and that she "had-it" and so I wasn't sure. I finally moved her and had her thoroughly detail the area which she did eagerly but never gave me her full trained indication. I saved the coordinates of the location on my GPS for my debrief report. At 1445 we existed the field. Debriefing was conducted, GPS tracks downloaded, gear stowed, dogs watered and kenneled for some well-deserved rest.

*The long hike out*

We didn't find Sammy. There were areas of interest by several of the teams, even a couple of canine alerts, but nothing definitive, nothing tangible, like a bone or even a button or a zipper. What's to say, however, that his spirit wasn't trying to communicate through the dogs, to us, as we hiked those many miles through a place known by the Native American tribes of the area as *giiwas*, a sacred place. The other thing that struck many of us was that even with the numerous signs of

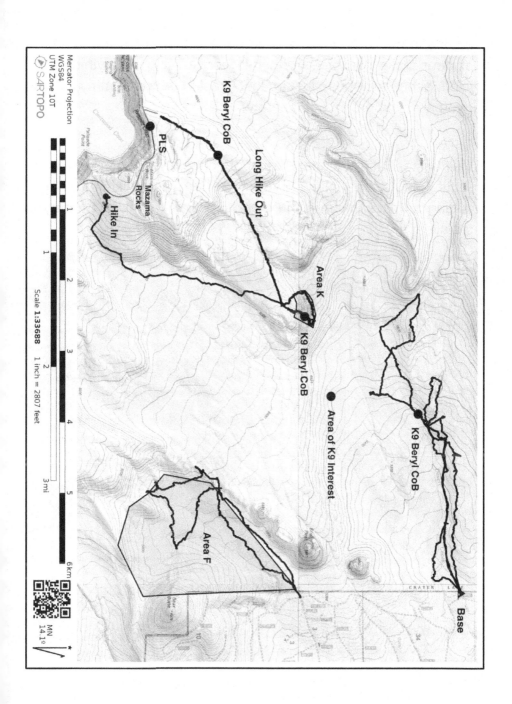

animal life in the area, there are no bones littering the forest floor, no elk or deer racks, no trace of anything once living. Everything is truly recycled, ashes to ashes, dust to dust. Rest in peace Sammy for where ever you are, you are loved by many.

----------

I visit Crater Lake National Park about once a year because it is such a beautiful and special place. Every time I am there hiking the trails or just sitting and breathing in the glorious vistas I think of Sammy and shed a silent tear.

*The phantom ship or ghost ship,*
*Crater Lake National Park*

# Two Days in Oso

It's been almost a week now since returning from Washington State and the disaster known as the Oso mudslide or as some would prefer it be called, the 530 slide. I will remember it always as the Oso mudslide, where in a minute's time on what would have normally been a beautiful spring day in 2014, 600 feet of bluff above the peaceful Stillaguamish River valley gave way destroying everything in its path. It's been estimated that 10 million cubic yards of mud and debris were unleashed across the river valley at speeds in excess of 60 mph. The date was March 22nd and the time was 10:37 am. Yes, it's true that WA State Route 530, a two-lane road that meanders peacefully through the valley, was washed away and covered in mud 30 to 50 feet deep; but I'd rather remember the slide for the small residential community on the outskirts of Oso known as 'Steelhead Haven' and the more than 42 souls (at least one person is still missing) that perished on that day, and not a road.

Neither my search dog Beryl, nor I, had ever worked a disaster callout. Disasters such as tornadoes, hurricanes, mudslides, terrorist attacks, are generally reserved for FEMA (Federal Emergency Management Agency) dogs. But until more FEMA dogs could be deployed to this disaster and after many of the local Washington SAR K9 Units had already been spent working on the site immediately after the slide occurred, the call went out for human remains detection dogs from nearby states: Oregon, California, Idaho, Montana, and even a Canadian province or two. We began the 10-hour drive north early on a Tuesday morning. Our SAR rig, a lumbering Chevy-Suburban, that drove more like a boat than a car, was packed full – two SAR canine's, myself, another canine handler, and two support personnel. Lucky, yes that is her name, was paired with me and we would share a tent, some late-night giggles, and a few tears during our deployment time.

Base of operations was the "Blue Grass" Fairgrounds in the small town of Darlington, just a few miles east of the slide. I had never been to this part of Washington and I can see why people have chosen to call this valley home. It's just beautiful. The forested mountains rise steeply to dizzying heights on either side of the river, jagged and snow covered, true sentinels, so close to the Seattle metropolis yet a million miles away. Upon arrival we got organized, reported in, and waited for the 1930 hours canine briefing. We were provided tents and a cot; meals, which we ate standing up, were being cooked by young men serving time in a correctional facility; a semi-trailer was equipped with hot water for showers, and the command structure was operating out of yurts – nicely labeled Communications, Logistics, Plans, Operations, etc. FEMA's Washington State Task-Force 1 was in Command but also nearing the end of their deployment and would hand over command to California Task-Force 7 out of Sacramento on Friday. And tucked in a corner of the fairgrounds, was a supply tent of donated items. Anything that you could need was there. Blankets, rain gear, gloves, duct tape, even toothpaste and soap was available; there was also a laundry service organized by the local community. This outpouring of support to assist us, the searchers, was amazing and something I will never forget.

Wednesday morning came early and dawned bright with hardly a cloud in the sky. After a hot breakfast, the order of the day was to meet at 0730 for a final canine briefing where our assignments would be confirmed, radios distributed, and any last-minute instructions given. We all met with gear ready, dogs at our sides. We were then loaded into vans and shuttled up to our work area. While I was there, there were two primary areas being searched (Area 1 and Area 4) and then some

*Lucky, Myself, and K9 Beryl ready to deploy*

canines were also being worked from small boats in areas still flooded. Beryl and I were assigned to Area 4 both days.

On that Wednesday, Beryl and I and Lucky were paired with a FEMA handler and his young chocolate Labrador named Kersey. We were the only canine teams assigned to Area 4 on this day. We were shuttled up the "power-line service road" to a series of white tents, our drop point. The road itself had literally been built in a day; providing both needed access to the slide and also connecting the west and east sides of the now bifurcated State Route 530. A local company had donated all of the rock and stone; something like 12 dump trucks full an hour had been poured along the hillside. Upon exiting the van, two things immediate played upon my senses. First, the noise from the heavy machinery operating everywhere – digging, moving, excavating – all the while the high-pitched whine of chainsaws buzzed in the background. The second was the scale of the slide and the unbelievable power of nature. It looked more like the aftermath of a volcanic eruption than a mudslide. Nothing was left standing in an area about 1 square mile. Geologists have called it a freakish-slide due to the scale, scope, and the slides' ferocity.

AJ, the FEMA handler assigned with me this day, had been on the slide for over a week already and gave me a quick ins and outs briefing. "Stay out of the black water," "try and walk on the darker shades of mud, the lighter colour stuff is mostly quicksand," "carry a stick as it will help you free yourself when you get stuck," "take your time, rest your dog often." We headed out together along a makeshift path of tress cut and stripped and laid in the mud to provide some access into the devastation, an actual skid road. There was a "pond" of black water to our left and Beryl immediately wanted to enter. She loves to work water. This is where I was thankful that I chose to be a little unconventional by having Beryl in harness and working her occasionally on a long biothane line. There wasn't much for her to get tangled on in our area and this way I could keep her safe and better direct her to specific areas to search. Plus, in regular training we do a lot of detail search work and she is used to working in harness and on a long line, so why mess with things now. As I stepped forward to extricate Beryl from the water, my left foot sunk in the mud over my knee. You really do get stuck. You can't move and you certainly can't pull your foot back out the way it went in but, if you bend your leg back at an angle of 90 degrees you can then lift it up and out of the muck. At least it worked this time and I was hoping not to have to test this theory again. Beryl kept trying to get into the water and worked with interest along the mounds edging the black water. Kersey was also showing interest. We marked this location, AJ called it in and a worker immediately arrived and placed two orange tip stakes in the mud where the dogs had interest, marking the area for the excavators to come dig. A little while later, we were again calling in a location and the area was similarly marked.

We took a rest out on the mud, next to a large American flag that had been raised earlier to half-mast and now flew symbolically over the expanse of destruction. As we rested, I pulled out the tube of Nutri-Cal that the vet staff was freely handing out that morning and Beryl was happy to lick up the instant energy from the tube. She even shared her tube with Kersey, who licked eagerly at the energy packed goo. We continued our efforts, Beryl working free now to explore the mud, the debris, to sniff out the odor that earns her a reward. And then she tried to cross the mud that looked like grits and she sunk up to her armpits, stuck in quicksand. I couldn't go in to help. Somehow Beryl was able to twist her body just enough that I could reach her harness and pull her to safety. I guess she hadn't been paying attention during the morning brief. Actually, one of the most difficult, challenging, and frustrating aspects of searching in this type of environment was that the dogs couldn't follow up on odor, couldn't work the drifting and swirling odor like they normally would as their path of travel seemed always thwarted by mud, stifling, sucking mud. It didn't matter the size or the will of the dog, the mud always won.

The dogs were getting tired, so we took a break and walked along another new gravel road to the base of a hill and a small section of the 530 that had been cleared and was accessible. We looked north across the road and there was nothing. It still wasn't safe to venture out there, so we just took a few moments lost in our own thoughts. Then we heard on the radio that a recovery was being made in our section. We walked back. One of the excavator operators had made a discovery beneath the mud. It was so near to where our canine's had shown their earlier interest. I believe they did have odor but couldn't go to final response as they could not access the precise location, the mud had won. At least that is what I wanted to believe, I wanted to feel like we were making some contribution in this utterly sad place.

Special crews donning white hazmat gear were summoned to remove the remains. Once on a stretcher, a long whistle was blown and everything went quiet. The National Guard met the stretcher and a transfer was done, a chaplain stood by, everyone was silent, every hardhat removed. It was beautiful. It still makes me a cry.

Canine shifts were typically four hours long, but we spent most of the day out in Area 4. As we were transported back down the mountain, I silently stared out the window, Beryl fast asleep on my lap while Kersey nestled up next to her on the bench seat of the van.

The next day was much the same. I was back in the same area paired with another FEMA handler, Lisa, and her dog Cody, a border collie-heeler mix. We were also assigned a safety officer. The area looked different, so much mud had been moved and rearranged. The black water filled pond was drained. We were asked to spot check a few areas. One of those areas was a small island of mud only accessible by crossing a log that had been placed above a muddy creek bridging one muddy bank to the other. Beryl alerted twice. The area was marked with the familiar orange tipped stakes; the area to be dug up later. I'll never know what if anything would be discovered at those locations. By mid-afternoon Beryl was getting tired. I let her rest in one of the warming

kennels. She fell asleep in seconds. It was time to head down the mountain to decontamination and then back to base.

'Decon' or decontamination was mandatory at the end of each day. Water stations (thankfully mostly warm water) were set up along the roadway and either National Guard or other volunteers would assist on washing the mud off of us and our K9 partners. Once back at base, I noticed Beryl was having trouble staying warm and was shivering. It had also started to rain. She spent probably an hour and half in a warming kennel that night and again Friday morning before we headed for home. Without the vet support, I have no doubt she would have been dog number 28 to suffer from hypothermia and need IV fluids.

Our time was over. It was short and the amount we contributed was infinitesimal but it still felt good. I'd do it all over again, but for now it was time to pack up the wet gear, tired dogs, and head home. CA Task-Force 7 had arrived Thursday night, half-dozen semi-trailer trucks full of gear. More FEMA canine teams were arriving from across the county. Our dogs were exhausted. We were too but hadn't really realized it until we got home where a week later, I still fell asleep exhausted.

----------

Oso took a lot out of Beryl. She was tired. That June we went back to Sisters, Oregon to recertify as a wilderness air scent team. She picked up the scent of Mack, our hider, almost immediately. But unlike how she and I together solved the scent puzzles in previous certifications, I could see now she was relying more on me to help. She

 started limping on her right front, her shoulder ached her. I got on the radio and called Mack and said, "it's over, she can't do this anymore." It was time for her to hang up her air scent shabrack, her vest that designated her as a search and rescue dog when we worked in the wilderness. Maybe we could continue to do some short less physically strenuous HRD searches. I was sad but deep-down I knew it was coming. We had already retired from agility competitions the previous year when she started to refuse the A-frame. I also had her eyes examined as something seemed "off," although no one could enlighten me on what or if there was a problem. She also started being more reactive to movement, vehicles in particular.

After failing our certification, we headed down to the annual CORSAR Summer-Exercise which was being held at Diamond Lake that year and hosted by Douglas County. I had taken to camping in my little teardrop trailer that I had built a few years prior, giving up the tent experience unless absolutely necessary. After sharing some wine with my good friend Lynda, who had a lovely mantrailing flat-coated retriever named Beezley, I hunkered down in my trailer with Beryl at my side and Tollie, my two-year old Sussex, at my feet. In the darkest hour of the night Beryl started kicking me. I whispered "stop," and then tried to nudge her over. She kept kicking. I flicked on the light and she was in the middle of a violent seizure. I didn't know what to do, so I just held her. It went on and on. Her bladder emptied. What was happening? Tollie, sensing something was wrong, snuggled up tighter. She finally went still and when she half opened her eyes she just looked blankly into space. She was so utterly confused; I was confused and my heart was breaking. I threw a clean blanket under her and then just held her tightly as we both slowly drifted back to sleep. There was nothing I could do now anyway. She awoke a bit groggy but otherwise seemed fine; she spent that day quietly resting in my trailer.

The following year, 2015, Summer-Ex was held at a place called Riley Ranch over on the coast. Lynda, Dave (with his German shepherd named Petey) and I caravanned over on a very pleasant Thursday afternoon and set up camp. As we drove over to the coast, however, I sensed something. The energy emanating from Beryl, felt off. The event started with all the canine teams in attendance being asked to respond to a search for an elderly-women with Alzheimer's just outside the little seaside town of Port Orford. I flanked for Lynda and K9 Beezley until the search was called off in the middle of the night due to a cougar sighting. The timing of that request to return-to-base couldn't have come at a worse time; both Lynda and I thought we heard something in the woods. We called out and listened but we only heard silence. Were we only imagining things? That night all tucked back into the trailer with the dogs, Beryl had another seizure. It had been a full year since the last one. That next morning with tears in my eyes and a heavy heart I packed up and headed home while the search for 78-year-old Joyce Huffman continued.

On Monday, Lynda and I with Beezley, Tollie, and Beryl, who had recovered and now seemed just fine, were back over at the coast. Joyce had still not been found. The search was winding down and this would probably be the last official search day. There were only a few other searchers out that day besides us; Lynda and I and Beezley and Tollie slashed our way through the thick coastal vegetation for most of the day with no sign of Joyce or any other clues. After debriefing we packed our rigs up and decided to get some fish and chips in Port Orford. We were just entering town when Lynda's phone rang and search managers requested us to come back to command. Joyce's red purse had been found! Beezley and Tollie were done for the day and to be honest so were we. I wanted to give it a shot though, so I got Beryl out of the car and put her bell on her collar signaling to her that we might be searching for someone no longer living. We headed straight for the purse while family members followed us. Beryl searched around the wooded area and then took off to the north – she had something. We followed and we emerged on a little dirt track, nothing but walls of gorse lining both sides of the narrow road for as far as we could see. I hesitated proceeding further because it was a road and I knew Beryl couldn't be around cars or ATV's or anything that moved. I decided that we should swing back the way we came to complete our loop of the area and then we ran into other searchers. I made myself believe that it was the other searchers she must have smelled anyway and I was tired and Lynda was tired and so I called it quits as soon as we completed the loop. I let her down again. I potentially let everyone down, Joyce most importantly.

*Joyce being comforted by SAR personnel after being found*

Jackson county's SAR Coordinator, Sergeant Shawn Richards asked me what I thought. I knew from reviewing the search map with over 4 days of search tracks depicted on it what had been searched and what hadn't and Beryl "did run north with purpose," so I suggested to the north of the purse and perhaps slightly westward. By the time we arrived home, Joyce had been found and she was miraculously alive! A ground search team had been sent north and west of the purse and a searcher skilled in mantracking noticed a human track leading into the gorse. They cut their way in and found Joyce who was only 750 feet north and slightly west of her purse.

Beryl's seizures started coming more frequently and after numerous tests she was put on phenobarbital. It helped tremendously, the seizures all but ceased. She deployed on a few HRD searches those last couple of years and she taught me a great deal about the discipline of detection. She learned the odor of firearms but we never got around to certifying. The training I believe kept her mind sharp and she was always up for little puzzle to solve. Her last official deployment was in March of 2017. That was the same day both Tollie and I were bitten by a tick that would have near dire consequences for one of us.

Beryl was a member of Josephine County Search and Rescue from 2006 – 2017. She certified to OSSA Standards as a Wilderness Air Scent Dog in 2008, 2010, and 2012, and as a Wilderness Human Remains Detection Dog in 2010, 2012, 2014, and 2016. She deployed on nearly 50 mission days. She never found anyone. She cleared areas, she provided important scent clues, some of which were used to assist in locating the missing or influencing the direction of a search while other potentially important scent clues were discounted even though she knew which way to go. She never lied and she never ever quit. Only her body quit.

She was diagnosed with cancer, hemangiosarcoma, on a Thursday in early November. I had noticed she was having trouble with rear-end strength, and figured it was that old horse injury acting up on her again. But it wasn't, it was cancer. Her body was riddled with it, she had even developed a heart murmur. She had probably been fighting it for years – little signs that I missed or discarded or explained away – not that I would have wanted to know. It was better this way. The weekend was

sunny and warm and we sat together for hours on the back porch. She couldn't control her bladder anymore and I made the call that following Monday, and we said goodbye to each other. I lost a piece of my heart when she passed.

On the way home from the vet's office, a full rainbow appeared in the sky. Thank you "little B," for being my first SAR partner, my very best girl.

Beryl was named after the famed aviatrix Beryl Markham, a strong woman with great spirit and a love for adventure. "Little B" was just like that, full of adventure and spirit. She is still the only Sussex spaniel to be certified in Wilderness Air Scent; she remains one of if not the most accomplished Sussex spaniels as well. She loved to work and she loved to play.

SAR K9 Beryl

Ch ShootingStar West w'the Nite, PCD, BN, RA, NA, NAJ, AXP, MJP2, MJPB, NFP, T2BP, SAR-W, CGC, TKI; Sussex Spaniel Ambassador Award, VEW, PDQ; ITD, NAC, NJC, NCO-1

(April 1, 2004 – November 13, 2017)

# CONNIE

"We who choose to surround ourselves
with lives even more temporary than our own,
live within a fragile circle; easily and often breached.
Unable to accept its awful gaps, we would still live no other way.
We cherish memory as the only certain immortality,
never fully understanding the necessary plan."
Irving Townsend

# Seeking Scent: My First Steps Into Mantrailing

Although Beryl was my first search and rescue partner, her dam Connie was my first ever dog. I grew up with cats. I learned about conformation dog shows with Connie and she earned her American Kennel Club (AKC) Championship, all owner-handled. I learned about bird hunting with Connie and she earned both her Working Dog Certificate from the American Spaniel Club and her AKC Junior Hunter Title. We did a little rally obedience together; she told me she hated it. I finally listened. She became a fabulous Therapy Dog, Canine Ambassador, and a K9-Reading Buddy. She whelped two amazing litters of puppies. One of her puppies was a dog named Tacker, owned by my good friends Penny and Terry. Tacker had a very successful show career including being a two-time National Specialty Winner, and winning Best of Breed at both the famous Westminster Kennel Club Dog Show and the AKC's National Championship Dog Show. And then, of course, there was Winston from her first litter and "little B," from her second litter. Connie was also was my first mantrailing dog.

The next two stories first appeared in the Sussex Scentinel, the newsletter of the Sussex Spaniel Club of America. This first story has been updated to reflect more of my current thinking on the discipline of mantrailing or, simply, trailing.

----------

Who said only bloodhounds can be mantrailers? I've been training my seasoned girl (read: pushing middle age) Connie in the discipline of trailing for the past year. It started out as more of a curiosity than really believing that we would ever be certified as a search and rescue canine team. After certifying Beryl in wilderness air scent, I really wanted to learn the trailing discipline and Connie really needed a job that was more physically and mentally stimulating than visiting schools and doing therapy work. Connie was to be my "training dog" but after just a few short months, it became clear that she had an innate aptitude for the discipline and she was physically strong enough to stand up to the rigors of wilderness terrain. So began our journey.

I suppose I should first explain that trailing is not the same as tracking although they do share commonalities. Tracking is defined as the propensity or learned ability of a dog to methodically follow the depositional odor/scent track (a complex combination of human scent, and odors emitted from ground disturbance and often crushed vegetation) by shaping the dog to work close to the footfall of the track layer; the dog should communicate to the handler to any dropped articles found along the way as well as following that track to its conclusion which could be an article or a person. The surface (vegetative or non-vegetative) on which the dog's foundational learning takes place will often influence the dog's olfactory focus. What odors does the dog find the most salient? Is it the odors of crushed vegetation, ground disturbance, the human scent component of the track, or some combination thereof?

Trailing can be defined as the propensity or learned ability of a dog to either follow the depositional track odor/scent picture and or the scent plumes associated with the missing person. The dog will use whichever search technique will get them to the missing person the most efficiently. While some trailing dogs may indicate on dropped articles, the dog's focus is to get to the end of the trail as quickly as possible since that is where they will find their quarry which is the goal of the hunt.

The focus of the search and rescue trailing dog then is to find the lost person in the most efficient means possible; if that means cutting a corner or air scenting then that is okay although during training, we do try to avoid setting up problems that routinely encourage those behaviours.  While some tracking dogs use a scent article to start, it is often not necessary; with a trailing dog it is critical in getting a good start.

*K9 Winston taking scent from the vehicle's door handle during a training exercise*

A scent article can be anything that has been exposed to and has absorbed the missing or lost person's unique scent profile. Materials that hold scent well, like fabrics or cloth, are ideal. Scent articles can also be made by transferring the person's scent from an item belonging or touched by them to an uncontaminated piece of cotton gauze. And lastly, scent articles can be something the person touched, like a car door handle; or perhaps simply a place a lost person sat down and rested, such as against a tall pine in the woods.

Trailing dogs also have to learn how to handle the fact that lost people often backtrack, walk in circles, or wander places that don't seem to make logical sense; the missing or lost also may be frightened, mentally unstable, confused, scared, injured or worse; and, they may have attempted to hide from the elements in makeshift shelters or just tucked themselves under a bush; so many scenarios to consider. Depending on environmental conditions, as a person walks, some scent will fall and/or be deposited directly on the path the person walked while some scent may be blown quite a distance from the actual path. The day's natural cycles of heating and cooling coupled with terrain will also

109

affect where and how the scent trail is dispersed while trail age and weather (temperature & humidity) will affect how much scent is available to the dog. Scent may pool in depressions tricking the dog into thinking that their quarry is near; the dog may pick up the scent on the wind from a considerable distance and now the dog needs to choose to either stay on the trail or try and "go more direct." Because there are so many variables affecting scent dispersion, the dogs are given the freedom to work the scent trail in a style that comes more naturally and more efficiently than precision tracking dogs. I like to think of a scent

trail as similar to how a river moves across the landscape; sometimes flowing straight and true as it cuts its way through rock; other times spreading its watery tentacles across a flat plan; and, all the while the water changes speeds, depths, eddies, warms and cools. Never think that trailing is just sloppy tracking or air scenting; it is neither, but instead a discipline unto itself. A beautiful discipline and one that Sussex are quite good at!

As far as to what discipline, trailing or air scent, the Sussex is more adept at, I think right now for me it's a toss-up. Beryl is an awesome little wilderness air scent dog, I think, however, that my next Sussex puppy will be started out as a trailing dog. I also still want someone to prove to me that there isn't some hound in these dogs! On the trail, I would swear I'm working behind a short legged, furry brown bloodhound. Determined, capable, and stubborn. Oh, and they can drool too!

*All smiles after K9 Connie passes her Intermediate-level certification*

----------

On February 17th 2009, Connie passed her intermediate-level wilderness trailing certification test and can join Beryl on mission callouts. For our county's intermediate-level test, her trail needed to be six-hours old and between ½ and 3/4's mile long (the actual trail was closer to 0.8 tenths of a mile long). And while it wasn't required at the time for the test to be conducted double-blind, in essence it was since a handler from out of county was brought in to conduct the evaluation and she had no prior knowledge of either the area or about where the trail would go or how it would end. Bless the trail layer who laid the trail in the dark so I could run it at a decent hour. I arrived near noon at the parking area and was briefed on the test exercise. The search scenario was that of a missing hiker that was last seen reading the historical marker down the road. My evaluator and I drove about a quarter-mile down the road and parked the car at the point-last-seen (PLS). I gathered my gear, harnessed Connie up while she waited patiently in the car and then presented her the scent article, a woolen hat owned by our missing person. When I ask her to "take scent," she sniffs the scent article and is then given a small treat; this a trick Janet taught me that she learned during that South Dakota seminar we attended and it really motivates the dog to take a good whiff. All of this was part of our starting ritual. After being released form the vehicle, she took a sip of water and, without hesitation, she pulled me along the road toward a gravel track. She circled the area briefly and committed to the old overgrown gravel track that headed uphill. There were three large earthen berms to negotiate first (these large mounds of dirt are used to deter off-road vehicles); as we topped the first berm below us was a large cold looking pool of grey chalk coloured water. I was oh so glad that instead of a cold swim she went around the water hole through the brush. Once successfully up and over the last berm, she picked up the pace as we continued uphill. As we crested the hill, the overgrown track opened up into a small clearing. It was obvious that the local kids had found this spot as discarded wine and beer bottles greeted our arrival. The main trail went off to the west along a ridge but Connie again confidently took a small game trail that ran northeast into the bush. She kept working with certainty into the thick bush (mostly manzanita) along a ridgeline. I use a biothane tracking line and I love it as it's doesn't get tangled or caught in the brush making it easy to drop and grab again after she has cleared the crud she is dragging me through. We encountered a small but very steep sided creek, and then more thick brush. My poor evaluator at this point ran into a tree and I could hear from behind me "OUCH, keep going I'm okay." Connie then turned westward and down off the ridge into a rocky "bowl" interspersed with some pine, tick-brush, and more manzanita. We crossed a smallish free flowing stream and then headed further down into the bowl along an old mining ditch before crossing both the ditch and the stream yet again. As we neared another gravel road, Connie picked up her pace and with a beautiful head-snap in the direction of the subject raced through the last of the manzanita and promptly sat in front of our subject. Connie ran the trail in a blistering

23 minutes. We were hauling and having a ball! My evaluator then checked the GPS readings and my missing person confirmed that she ran a really tight trail which was what she was indicating to me all along. A very confident little brown dog for sure.

Connie's next level of certification will be to test to the Oregon State Sheriffs Association (OSSA) standards. Wish us luck!

----------

Connie passed her OSSA trailing evaluation in June 2009. She was 10 years old and is the only one of my three mantrailing dogs to pass the OSSA trailing certification as the standards were written in the day. I am pretty proud of her for that.

*Connie finding Sue and passing her benchmark evaluation*

*OSSA Standard. Track/trail a person, not known to handler or dog, that has walked at least 1.5 miles in moderate to rough terrain. An uncontaminated scent article will be provided the handler at the start of the evaluation. The track will be allowed to age overnight a minimum of 12 hours. The dog must be able to take scent from the article and start the track/trail. The dog must work through natural occurring contamination and distractions. The handler must recognize if/when the dog is off the track/trail. At the end of the track/trail the dog must find and take the handler to the subject at the end of the trail. Subject must be located to pass the test.*

# A Day Well Spent

At least once a year, Josephine County Search and Rescue conducts a mock search exercise; real-world training to keep us sharp. This was to be Connie's first such exercise since becoming certified as a wilderness trailing dog by the Oregon State Sheriffs Association. I want to share the story of our search exercise because to me, Connie (and Beryl), demonstrate the best working qualities of our breed: *"the Sussex was developed to work as a methodical, determined, thorough hunter, with a moderate pace, excellent endurance and an overall toughness."*

The search exercise was very realistic in many ways. First was the location. The search planners chose for our exercise a stretch of rugged land along the Illinois River, a major tributary of the Rogue River. Most of the river has been designated a Wild and Scenic River and both the river and the surrounding area, the Kalmiopsis Wilderness, is popular

*Looking downriver from the "Green Bridge"*

with hikers, hunters, and river rafters. Over the years, this area has seen numerous search and rescue missions, and sadly some recovery operations.

The morning of the exercise, I woke to cloudy skies and light drizzle. A sight far better than the previous days hard rain. After arriving on site and being briefed on the exercise scenario – three, maybe four, overdue gold panners (yes, there is still gold in them thar hills!) – I received my assignment. I was assigned to start with my trailing dog, Connie, from the last-known-point (LKP) to see if we could determine a direction of travel of the "missing persons." The LKP was a vehicle which was parked at the side of the road at a place known by the locals as the "Green Bridge," because, well, the steel bridge is painted green. A dirt track heads west from the bridge and parallels the river for several miles. The area around the vehicle was taped off to preserve any available clues, like a footprint. Unfortunately, because of the narrowness of the road, the only place the mounted unit could stage their horses safely while waiting for their assignment was on the dirt track adjacent to the vehicle; so much for a footprint or an uncontaminated area to start working.

I brought Connie over to the car, opened the passenger side of the car (the side I was instructed to open; remember this was a pre-planned exercise) and asked her to take scent from inside the car. I also collected a scent article from the car just in case I needed to refresh her olfactory memory while out on the trail; there was a baseball cap on the dashboard and also several items on the passenger seat of the car including a pair of socks, which I ultimately selected. Enter the next real-world scenario: a bad scent article.

Connie immediately went to work and pulling into her harness we headed north up the very rutted dirt road. Rain water filled pot holes which were so deep that she had to swim along the road in places, my flanker Kate and I wading along behind while our boots sunk into the clay muck below. Connie continued to work along this lower road paralleling the river, checking a couple of times down along the river where scent had been transported on the wind. She continued along the wet muddy road for approximately ½ mile before turning upslope through the pine trees and thick brush. About half way up the slope my flanker asked us to stop so she could shed some layers of clothing;

115

even though it was chilly and damp out, our pace was quick enough to warm us up. Connie was not interested in water or resting and waited impatiently by pulling in her harness. A little further up the slope and Connie again changed direction and pulled us through thick manzanita and crimson coloured poison oak until we entered an old placer mining area. This old mining area was fascinating with large rock tailings, water scoured ravines, scrub brush and exposed rock, the entire area painted in numerous shades of gray and red.

The mining area was also more exposed to the wind which was at our backs and being funneled northward and accelerating along the river canyon. In one location, Connie had to circle several times before committing to the north again. As we continued further into the mining area, Connie's body language changed and her pace quickened, indicating one of our subjects was near. We next found ourselves at the bottom of a 50-foot-high pile of smooth water washed rocks. Without

hesitation, Connie advanced up the rock pile as Kate and I watched our every step so as to not slip, twist an ankle, or worse. When we reached the top,

Connie stopped and then took us down the pile of rocks toward the river. She then tried to parallel the river heading back south but we hit an impenetrable blackberry thicket and an unstable tailing pile. I knew we were close but we just couldn't seem to flush out our subject.

After circling the northern end of the old tailing area, we ended up on the upper main dirt access road. Several vehicles passed us with ground teams headed out to their assigned search area. Connie continued north along the main dirt access road searching but it soon became very clear that she had lost the trail. In hindsight, I should have taken her back into the mining area one more time but as we were close to a campground at the far end of the road, I suggested that we go into the campground area and work her there and see if she cuts a trail out of the campground. Sure enough, she did pick up scent and started taking us up the steep rock and brush covered slope of Eight Dollar Mountain toward a place on the map labeled Faye's Gulch. At this point I admit to starting to doubt her a bit as I knew other searchers were in the area although she didn't appear to be paying them any attention. I'll never know what would have happened as it was about this time that we were radioed to return to command for another assignment. We had been out for nearly two hours and had traveled well over three miles.

First though was a thorough debriefing in the comforts of an old Army bus. I suggested, based on what Connie was communicating to me through her body language, that a ground team needed to search the northern end of the mining area more thoroughly. Sure enough, a team was sent into the area, and the car's owner, Greg, was found hunkered down along the river just a few hundred feet to the south of where Connie was turned back by the blackberries and the unstable tailing pile.

Kate, as my flanker, and I then headed back out on another assignment. I first switched dogs, as this was a training problem for Beryl, one of our team's air scent dogs. We were asked to complete the search assignment, an area of about 100 acres, initially given to the mounted unit. The terrain proved to be too dangerous for the horses and several pasterns had been cut on the hillsides sharp rocks before they were forced to abandon their search efforts due to safety. My plan was to climb to the highest portion of the search area and then grid down the slope and into the wind as best as possible.

So, we headed up the grass covered rocky slope. At about the 1,600-foot level (200 feet shy of the uppermost portion of the search area),

Beryl started to work south and it was clear she was in scent. She continued along at 1,600 feet, checking thickets along the way, as if she could read the contour lines on a map and took us directly to the missing subject. Turns out, the subject stayed at 1,600 feet all the way

*K9 Beryl finding the training subject and earning a treat*

into his hiding spot. We were in and out of the area in about 45 minutes. It was a day well-spent along one of the most beautiful rivers and in one of the most beautiful spots of southern Oregon.

After the search exercise was over, I discovered some interesting facts. Remember those socks that I collected from the vehicle as a scent article; well, turns out that they were not even one of the lost subjects but those of a family member and had been laundered the day before and had just been sitting in the car overnight. And Greg, the person Connie was so determined to find had actually gotten a ride in a quad up the dirt track for the first 1/4 mile! I also learned that the baseball cap that was on the car's dashboard was placed there by Brian, another of the missing, and he had begun his hike to his hiding spot in Fayes Gulch by walking along the same dirt road. The third subject never went near the vehicle and was the person located by Beryl in the area southeast of the LKP, the opposite direction from the direction Connie worked.

I have no doubt that Connie knew that two people had been in the car when she "took scent;" that she trailed Greg (the car's owner) to the northern end of the mine area where he was found by a ground team and that she picked up Brian's scent when we headed upslope from the campground in the direction of Faye's Gulch. I also believe both girls exhibited those working traits that we strive for in our Sussex spaniels:

*"Methodical, determined, thorough hunter, with a moderate pace, excellent endurance, and an overall toughness."*

*K9 Connie trailing through the mine tailings*

# Starry, Starry Night

Since Connie got a late start in life as a search and rescue dog, Connie and I only deployed on a few actual missions. The search for little 4-year-old Zoey Dorsey search outside of Brookings being the most memorable but not for the expected reasons. My husband, Dave, and I were at the local cinema watching the new Alice in Wonderland movie when my pager started to vibrate. Oh darn. The movie was thankfully just ending and we hurried out into the lobby to use the cinema phone so I could get the details. A missing child.

As soon as we got home, I got me gear organized and Dave printed me a couple of rudimentary Google-maps so I could find the home in the dark (for my Birthday the following month, Dave surprised me with a car GPS that I still have and use to this day). Brookings is a coastal community about a 1 ½ hour drive along some mighty twisty and narrow roads from Grants Pass. I followed the directions and arrived at the house, perched high on a hill overlooking the city of Brookings and vast swaths of steep forested slopes at about 8 pm; it was very quiet, except for the wind rushing in from the sea up into the mountains. Stars filled the dark sky; a sliver of a crescent moon and a faint glow of city lights far below eliciting a sense of loneliness.

The command vehicle was set up and Janet and K9 Angie with support were already out searching but most of the other searchers hadn't arrived yet from what I could tell. I went to check in and get briefed and things were so early in the game that the maps I brought from home were taken from me to use for search planning. I didn't receive an assignment and so I just sort of waited around. I was a little confused, the small girl had been missing 5 hours at this point, why no assignment?

Searchers started dribbling in and with no good place to park, the narrow driveway up to the house became choked with vehicles, limiting a good view of the surroundings. A dirt track that led off to the east was blocked by cars and hidden in the darkness; I certainly never noticed it that dark night. Janet and K9 Angie and the rest of the trailing team returned to base empty-handed. I still had no assignment but thanks to Janet, who stuck her head into the Command Post and mentioned a fresh certified canine had arrived to assist, I was ultimately asked to take Connie out to check some areas where Angie had some "interest." Janet and Peggy, from Del Norte County, served as my support. By the time we got started it was after 9 pm.

It was requested that I drive down the road about ¼ mile and start my search efforts from there. I secretly wished I could begin at the house. I also wasn't afforded an opportunity to collect a scent article, so used a pillow that Janet had collected earlier. I felt confident in our skills but we were new to the trailing discipline and the assignment seemed makeshift. Of course, if it hadn't been for Janet suggesting we be given an assignment, I'm not sure I ever would have received one. Connie initially headed downhill toward a house at a "T" junction in the road. The house appeared vacant. She circled the house, discounting the back of the house but sniffed intently at the front of the house, her nose glued to the baseboards and the front door of the house. We checked the doors and they were all locked. Connie then worked west down a common driveway; I think it was Janet who informed me that they had headed that way as well and the residents were only marginally cooperative. She suggested that "Maybe we should turn around?" I was concerned that Connie was following where Angie and Janet had already checked due to a contaminated scent article.

I made the decision to restart further down Mountain Drive, where Janet and Angie had not searched. Connie's focus and energy notably changed. As she reached the corner with Canyon Drive, she did a huge shake-off and then checked the right side of the road. There was a drain culvert with water flowing through it; she then raised her head and it was clear she was in strong scent. She circled the corner frantically. I knew from my training that she did this when she encountered a scent pool of who she was looking for. She also tried to climb a 20-foot-high embankment. Now, Missy Connie wasn't going to expend anymore energy that necessary so for her to do something so out of the ordinary was important. We found a way up the dirt embankment where we searched the woods that made up the undeveloped intersection of Mountain and Canyon Drive. While she searched, she appeared to have lost the scent she had just encountered. Peggy was getting tired and I think sort of losing faith in our abilities and wanted to head back. I never did work up Canyon Drive. We headed back to Command. It was 11 pm.

In my debrief, I noted the wind was potentially making it difficult for my dog to really lock onto a trail. And it was windy that night with gusts over 20 mph. I did suggest that a Deputy double check the locked and vacant house and I did report and suggest that the area around the intersection where Mountain and Canyon Drives met be searched again.

After returning to base and debriefing, I asked for another assignment. Could I do more? A team of Josephine County searchers were about to deploy along an old track on the west side of the property and I asked if I could join them and bring Connie. "Yeah sure," was the response from Command. So, four Josephine County searchers, myself and Connie set-off to work along the track and hopefully maybe Connie would pick up scent again. Connie showed no interest along this road.

We began our efforts at 2 am and searched until 0430 in the morning. I drove home just as light broke on the eastern horizon.

I arrived home and caught up on some sleep. When the call came to head back over for more searching, I chose to stay home. The lack of organization, wasteful use of resources left me with a bad taste in my mouth. Many trained resources just weren't being used well; things were disorganized. In a press article written shortly after the search, it was satisfying to see the mistakes acknowledged so improvements could be adopted.

*"Last week Bishop and his immediate team met with some 40 other law enforcement members from the other counties who participated in the search and rescue at a meeting in Medford. There would be things Bishop would have done differently if it had to be done again. Bishop said he would have had more incident command people present, and he wouldn't have set up incident command so close to the Dorsey's home. Having the incident command at the end of the road made it difficult to process search volunteers. Bishop said more than 200 volunteers participated, but it was tough getting them all through, and others gave up and either went home or out on their own searches."*

Thankfully, little Zoey was found alive that afternoon just after 5 o'clock by two Brooking's citizen searchers or what have become to be known as emergent volunteers. She was located just off the dirt track that ran on the east side of the house and only a few hundred yards from her home. This was the same dirt track that was blocked by vehicles that first night. She was all but invisible, tucked into thick coastal vegetation. The citizen volunteer, Robert Crump, commented that he heard a whimper, a funny yip noise, and began searching through the tangled brush, *"She was so buried and camouflaged under the stickers and salal. I was circling around these bushes. I was very close but didn't realize it. And then I found her! I got her picked up and put her arm around my neck and she latched onto me. It was a miracle I found her."*

123

The search for Zoey was one of the largest search and rescue missions ever in Curry County and involved hundreds of volunteers throughout the State. Of course, after the search concluded, I studied my maps and tried to understand Connie's clear behaviour change of being in scent in relation to where little Zoey had been found. From my notes:

After analyzing where Zoey was located and where Connie showed interest, I do believe that she was "in-scent" of the little girl but not on her actual path. Based on my understanding of where the subject was located and analyzing the wind direction and terrain features, I believe Connie hit a scent pool of the subject when she reached the intersection with Canyon Drive which was just down the ravine/slope and downwind from where Zoey was located. A culvert with flowing water is also at this location. Wind and water both excellent medians for scent distribution. Distance from intersection to subject location was approximately 1/3 mile.

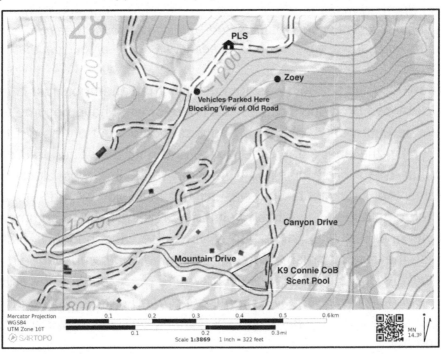

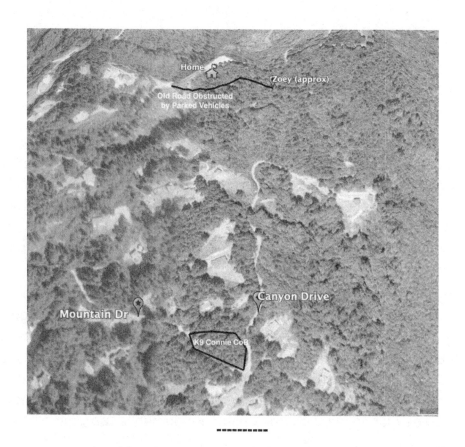

---

A month later we headed over to Sprague River in Klamath County for another search for child; it also thankfully ended successfully but was equally as frustrating from a canine handler's point of view. This would have been a perfect search for Connie but a trailing dog had already worked from the little boy's house and had come up empty so there was no use for "a second opinion." I was clearly the new kid on the block. Beryl, at least, got an assignment, but it was quite frustrating to have a well-trained dog and then not be asked to search. I'm sure these two searches planted the seeds that would emerge later in my SAR career as I undertook training in Search Management, focusing on mission planning.

# A Hot Summers Day

Connie's final search mission happened in late July of 2010. Rather than a wilderness setting, this time we would be searching a city setting. As often happened on mutual assist callouts, we would get a stand-by page. That happened in this case and the first page came at 0130. I slept fitfully after that and then another page at 0330 requesting we meet at the SAR house at 0530 before caravanning the 50 or so miles to the town of Ashland in neighboring Jackson County.

Ashland is a quaint little town and world renowned for its Shakespeare Festival and the plays that are put on almost year around. This search would actually begin in front of the main theatre on S. Pioneer Street which backed up to beautiful Lithia Park. Kevin Nay, 50 years old, was in town with his parents that Sunday evening and the family was going to take in a play, *Henry IV Part One*. A few years prior, Kevin was diagnosed with frontotemporal dementia, an umbrella term for a group of brain disorders that primarily affect the frontal and temporal lobes of the brain. These areas of the brain are generally associated with personality, behaviour, and language. The disease causes these areas to be to atrophy. As the family walked toward the front of the theatre, Kevon walked ahead and then disappeared into the crowd. It was 8 pm on a very warm evening, temperatures still hovering in the lower 90's.

By the time we arrived on scene at 0600 in the morning, Kevin had been missing already 10 hours. The night before, K9's and ground teams had canvassed the area immediately around where Kevin was last seen with no luck or clues to report. Search efforts also focused around Lithia Park because it was reported "he liked to visit parks."

Upon arrival at command, Connie and I were asked to deploy to the point-last-seen (PLS) and try and pick up a trail. It was cooler but still 70 degrees and the air still dry. Under another cloudless sky it was going to heat up fast. I immediately deployed to the PLS to see if we could pick up a trail. My flanker was my friend Denise who was training a lovely golden retriever, Cody, for wilderness air scent. She had assisted me just the week before in northern California along the Klamath River where Beryl and I worked in the blazing heat, among rattlesnake infested rocks, for a man who had been missing for over a month. Denise penned the below article about that Klamath River search which was posted to the Josephine County SAR blog.

----------

*"You have to start somewhere. I was anxious to put my training into practice, and this search was supposed to be a half day, not that far away, AND I'd be in the capable hands of my team leader, Ann McGloon. What could be so hard about that?*

*I drove through the predawn coolness to Ann's residence, a half hour from mine, possible scenarios playing themselves to different endings in my mind. Wouldn't it be awesome to be the ones to find our subject?! Timing was perfect, Ann's little red car (that could, we'd find out later) was packed and dog ready. I slung my gear behind the seat and we were off to meet the rest of SAR in the parking lot in Talent as the eastern sky turned gray.*

*Our caravan complete, five vehicles snaked onto I-5 and our adventure continued onward, Ann filling me in on search protocols, what to watch for with the dogs and heat, and what conditions we could expect. Not far from Hornbrook, along the Klamath River, the sun's rays lit the mountain tops towering above us, as the road went from paved, to gravel, to rocky rutted dirt. Ann gripped her wheel and crawled forward over boulders and dips. I held my breath, and prayed we'd be ok as things went from bad to worse. At one point she stopped the car and we stepped out to assess the situation. Dave (our SAR coordinators husband) took the wheel and we pressed onward, the sun's rays spiking through tree limbs causing me to squint to see the way. Actually, too far onward; we had to turn around and backtrack a short way to command,*

The horrible road to Command.

set up in a vast meadow surrounded by towering rock faced cliffs, conifers and oaks.

Ann and Monica parked a short way away from the bustle under shady pines to cool the dogs. By the time we stepped through an old wire fence, command had been set up, and a helicopter arrived on scene. The persons in charge conferred and we had a briefing. Turns out the helicopter was available to airlift us volunteers to hospitals if we were bit by any of the numerous rattlesnakes in the area. We were given photos of the missing person, his car, and the snakes. The air quickly went from comfortable to bake as I shrugged on my pack full of water and V8 juice, and rolled up the sleeves of my uniform shirt.

Monica gathered her team: Doug (first search for him as well!!! Yea, Doug!!!), Ken, and Joan. I was on Ann's team along with Paul and Jeff. We set GPS coordinates and hit our areas as the heat index went up a few more degrees. Finally, I was actually searching for someone! Every rock, log could have his remains tucked next to it, or maybe over there, under the tick brush? I have to admit, I kept an equally vigilant eye out for the rattlesnakes. I even hoped to at least see one from a distance. Better yet, to find this missing man, who was determined enough to get to his destination, that he buried his low-slung car in the mud, he had to be determined after our "cruise" up that remote road in DRY conditions. Was his family aware of our search? Were they hoping for answers, at last?

Word of bones found. We sprayed Beryl with water and adjusted a cooling vest on her, and led her to the area that now was sweltering with heat. The little brown dog did as trained, and we knew it wasn't our man. Beryl's efforts earned her a mass of burrs, seeds and stickers caught in her coat. Back up the dusty road to her car, and I offered water and combed out the worst of the mess.

*Our team went out on one more grid and searched as the sun stood high in the sky. I found myself going from shade to shade, pausing to check all around me, still hoping that someone today would make the find. Somewhere around one we were done, feet hot, shirts sticking, and water low. Our GPS tracks were downloaded, and we made ready to leave. Temp was 106.*

*Ann and I were a bit quieter on the way home, adrenaline rush over, and myself sorting through the experience. Yes, it was worth it, and yes, I'd gladly do it again."*

*Denise helping to keep K9 Beryl cool*

And she would. Denise and K9 Cody had a long and admirable career with Josephine County SAR.

----------

Connie steadily worked the "gathering area" in front of the theatre, she checked a now empty parking garage, her behaviour changed a bit as she checked several store fronts on main street and finally, we circled back to where the shuttle bus had reportedly dropped the family off in front of the theatre. We headed uphill, much of Ashland is a very hilly city, and ended up behind the theatre; it felt like she had finally locked on to a trail. We were now in Lithia Park and she was working quickly and with purpose ignoring the yoga class that was just breaking

129

up. She exited the park and crossed busy Granite Street and headed up a lane lined with beautiful homes. Strawberry Hill was the name of the street. As we crested the top of the steep hill, a 600-foot elevation gain from the cool grass and trees of the park below, she was pooped and had started to lose the scent trail. It was now already in the 80's and the asphalt was getting hot. She wouldn't stop though and to think that just a week and half earlier she had been in the hospital for two days on IV fluids getting over a GI issue that was never really pinpointed but was suspected to be a severe case of gastroenteritis. We finally stopped and rested and I gave her water which she reluctantly drank; assuming we were done, I tried to return the way we came but Connie was having none of it. She insisted that we continue and who was I to argue with that Sussex determination and perseverance. Finally, she lost it. As we descended back toward Command, we found some irrigation canals that bordered Hald/Strawberry Park and she got a nice welcomed cool down as she waded through the canals. It was now near 90 degrees and she had worked for near 3 hours.

Just as we finished our debrief, I heard over the radio that there had been an unconfirmed sighting on Strawberry Hill Rd; reports were also coming in of other reported sightings in other parts of town. The fliers and the public were starting to provide some much-needed clues. Then just a few minutes before 11 that morning, the good news searchers always are hoping for, Kevin had been found! What was amazing was where he was found, some 10 miles outside of town on Highway 66 which heads up into the Cascade Mountains. A Mail Tribune photo editor and a reporter on their way to an assignment elsewhere noticed Kevin walking along the narrow and twisty mountain road. They reported that Kevin initially denied that he was even lost but he fit the description on the flier released that morning by the police. So, they showed him the copy of the photograph and asked "Is that you?" and Kevin responded "That's me." Kevin explained later that he had walked all night but didn't recall or couldn't explain where he had been or where he was going.

----------

Connie did get to search one last time after she retired in the summer of 2011 when she turned 12 years old. Sara, our SAR Coordinator called, and asked if I could help an Ashland family find their lost dog. The family had been camping over the Fourth of July weekend up at Lake of the Woods and when the fireworks started their golden retriever was spooked and ran off into the woods. It had been several days and they had searched and searched and were desperate for help. "Well, it won't hurt to give it a try," I responded and called the family to see if we could help. My husband Dave came to follow along with me. I had never done anything like this before and so suggested that the family bring with them something that belonged to the dog so Connie could get a good whiff. They brought her harness. We met up near some cabins where there had been a possible sighting of the dog.

I scented Connie on the harness and followed Connie as she worked up around the cabins eventually moving closer to the lake and through an old girl scout camp. Her paced picked up and next thing we knew we were at a cabin. Connie climbed the stairs and sniffed all around the cabin exterior. The trail ran cold here. The owners who were following us told me "this is where we stayed!" I said, I think she is nearby probably hiding like scared dogs will often do when they are lost. I suggested when it was dusk or dawn to just sit outside near the cabin and watch and listen.

Dave and I headed home. The next day I received a call and the lost dog was back home with its family. The owners had done just as I suggested that evening and sure enough at dusk their dog wandered into view and there were able to coax her in. A happy ending. The pup had been missing for over a week.

Sometime that year, I don't recall exactly when Connie suffered a vestibular episode. Scared me to no end. While she was recovering, wobbly head and jiggering eyes, Connie never missed a meal. She was like that. Strong, determined. She got bit by a rattlesnake one summer and while her face puffed up a bit, she showed no other ill effects. I suspect a dry bite, but still. She was amazing. The last year or two of her life she started to show signs of severe cognitive decline. On more than one occasion she stumbled into our property fence but couldn't back up; she fell into a hole and couldn't extricate herself; she tried to walk through an iron fence and got stuck. Actions we often see from people suffering from Alzheimer's. One summer day in 2015, just before turning 16, Connie looked at me with her brave eyes and said "I have had enough!" I knew the look; my mother had given me the same look the evening she passed. She told me she had no regrets, loved her life, but it was time to go. Darn, I hope I am that strong when the time comes.

SAR K9 Connie

Ch Stonecroft Cosenza, JH, RN, WD, CGC, TDInc., Reading Buddy, AKC Canine Ambassador, VW, PD, ROM, Sussex Ambassador Award

(June 6, 1999 – June 29, 2015)

# WINSTON

"There is a beautiful thing inside you
that is thousands of years old.
Too old to be captured in poems.
Too old to be loved by everyone.
But loved so very deeply by a chosen few."
Nikita Gill

Oh Winston, my sweet old Winston. Winston was one of Connie's pups from her first litter and was born in April of 2002 when we lived outside of Washington D.C. in northern Virginia. At 10 weeks, his new family picked him up and off he went to live the life of a well-loved family companion in New York. Then life happened, a second baby was born and it all became too much so Winston needed a new home. He remained in New York with friends of his first family. Then I received a call from our Sussex Breed Rescue committee that the owners of Winston did not want him anymore. When I called the family, they told me *"he grabbed one of the children's arms and that he likes to sit in the rain by himself on the deck, we need him gone!"* While talking to the owner, all I could hear was the chaos of children running and screaming in the background, I wanted Winston out of there too. So, I made arrangements to bring him home to me in Oregon. As he was going for his veterinarian check, a woman in the waiting area took a liking to him and next thing I know we are having a series of conversations about Winston staying in New York. Winston was rehomed yet again, this time settling into an apartment along New York's 5th Avenue, going to doggie day care and generally living a nice quiet life. His owner, however, was travelling too much so in May 2009, at age 7, Winston finally made his way back home to me.

I drove up to Portland International Airport and picked Winston up over in the cargo section of the airport. He jumped right into my car and settled in for the four-hour ride home. He laid down and never raised his head until about an hour and half from home. The windows were partially down as it was a warm day and as we rounded a large bend in the road along the South Umpqua River, a herd of cows lazily eating lush green spring grass, he raised his head and then sat up and looked around. I still call this bend in the road "Winnie's corner." He was finally home.

*Welcome home Winston! Our first hike together was at Applegate Lake. I think he looks pleased.*

Winnie fit into my pack easily but was a bit of a loner. He often seemed a little lost, a little sad and forlorn. He reminded me of Eeyore from the Winnie the Pooh stories. He was wise, soulful, a beautiful little dog. One day in November of that year, I found myself over at the coast for a bit of training. I brought Winnie with me so he could enjoy a ride to the coast and maybe a walk along the beach. For the fun of it at the end of training I asked if someone would mind playing the runaway game with Winnie. "I think he might find it fun," I said. Oh, he found it more than fun. Age seven is really no time to start a SAR dog but when my plans for a new pup that summer fell thru, I thought "why not, I had the time," I told myself.

In October of the following year Winnie passed his intermediate-level certification making him mission ready by our county-standards. His first search didn't come until the following spring when he was approaching nine years old.

In the two plus years that Winston served as my canine partner, he proved himself quite a remarkable little dog. He gave everything, every time. We deployed together only on about a dozen searches but they were some of the best times and some of the most stretching times; physically connected by a thin piece of biothane but emotionally connected by something much stronger. He taught me more about the science and the art of mantrailing than I could have imagined. Was he perfect? Of course not. He multi-tasked at times, scarfing discarded food (an apple, a banana, a hot dog, or a cow pie) lying along his path as he tracked with purpose never missing a beat. He also taught me a great deal about scent, a dog's capabilities and also the possibilities.

*Top: K9 Winston on trail*
*Lett: Always ready to run a trail*
*Right: Finding Denise hiding in a feed box*

# Six Days

March 2011. The call came on Monday afternoon while I was at agility class with Beryl and Winnie. Elijah, a young man from California had been reported missing by his family and they had expressed grave concern for his well-being and mental health, according to the report from the Oregon State Police (OSP). We were asked to help find him. For the next two days, Josephine County Search and Rescue scoured the east side of the freeway adjacent to Interstate 5's northbound Manzanita Rest Stop where Elijah's abandoned car had been discovered. The busy rest stop is just outside the small town of Merlin where our SAR headquarters building, affectionately referred to as "the barn," is located so we didn't have far to travel for this search. On Tuesday, five canines and a large contingent ground searchers spent the day scouring the area for any sign of the missing.

I had both K9 Winnie, my trailing dog, and K9 Beryl, my wilderness air scent and human remains detection dog, on hand that day. While ground searchers and the other K9 teams deployed, I waited for a scent article to arrive from California and was briefed again by the OSP officer in charge. The last probable citing of Elijah had been six days earlier at the freeway rest stop. "Six days," I thought. I explained to the officer that my dog and I would do our best but six days is an old trail, the weather had been stormy for the last week with high winds and heavy rainfall, and the contamination of the scene — thousands of cars and their occupants pulling in and out of this busy rest stop — would make it extremely difficult if not impossible to pick a trail up and determine a direction of travel. I wasn't holding out much hope. Win and I had never trained on such an old trail and the area was now further contaminated with the fresh scent of familiar ground searchers and K9 teams as they canvassed the area.

A short while later, another OSP trooper pulled in and retrieved a large box from the trunk of his car, walked over to my vehicle placed the box down and went back and sat in his police car. The scent articles had arrived. The box was full of items belonging to Elijah. With gloved hands, I carefully opened the box and extracted a pillow case. Once Win was harnessed my flanker and I were ready to give it a try. I had already decided to not start Win where the car had been abandoned but instead decided to work him around the perimeter of the rest area along a concrete barricade where Elijah's scent might have collected and where it might remain. I leaned over and showed Win the pillowcase and whispered, "take scent, find'em," and Win immediately began circling. He then pulled me directly to the trooper's vehicle, the one who had just delivered the box of belongings, and jumped up with his front paws on the car's hood. Cross contamination? "Nope, not him Win," as I presented the scent article again and caste him in a larger circle. Win then went to check out another Officer who was standing near his vehicle but his body language immediately said, "not him."

With all the people in our immediate area checked off some mental list in Winnie's head, my brown dog started searching along the concrete barrier that encircled the east side of the rest area. He put his paws up on the top of the barricade several times and tried to jump over. On the other side was a small irrigation ditch filled with water. We found a way over the wall and Winnie started working along the irrigation ditch and heading north. He was working quickly, pulling hard into the harness, zigzagging through the heavy brush as he crossed several small creeks and trotted across wet muddy ground. To me, he seemed to be working too fast and I knew searchers had just been through the area. "Had he jumped trail?" I wondered. We passed by a trash-strewn transient camp but after a quick sniff of some of the debris, he gave it no notice. We then existed out of the thickest brush and into a clearing where a stream flowed west under the freeway. I had my flanker check the drainage pipe as best he could, nothing. I saw searchers about ¼ mile away standing on a hill and still wondered "if Win was on the correct scent." I scented him again.

Win continued north paralleling the freeway. I was thankful for the wire fence that also paralleled the freeway; Win stayed right on the fence-line as we headed north, huge semi-trucks barreling past us just a few feet away. I held the line tight. He gave the trucks no notice. We now had passed the searchers and Win had taken us to a road (again paralleling the freeway) that entered Sportsman's Park, the local gun club. A car passed us by. Then a few seconds later, Win's head went up in the air like it does when he captures the scent of who he is following; he pulled toward the hill to our east. I marked the position on my GPS. He circled a bit and then headed up the road following the speeding car. Did Win think that the missing was in that vehicle? I was losing confidence. The car had stopped at the gun club's office and Win went over to the two gentleman that had been watching us, sniffed them, and then with his body language he signaled "not him."

We told the gentleman who we were looking for and asked if the hillside, where Win's head had raised, was clear to search. It was part of the archery course and we were assured no one was out today. As we took Win back down the road, he showed mild interest along one corner of the gun club's small pond where it linked to the pond's out-take. H'm. Win then worked up the steep hillside to the east but when we crested the hill, his interest faded. I told my flanker that I think if he had it, he lost it, but inside I'm not even convinced he ever had it. We walked back down to the road. I started to turn back south toward the rest-stop and Win planted his butt in the middle of the road and looked north not budging. "Okay, so where Winnie?" I scented him yet again.

Winnie then headed off the road and back through the brush toward the freeway. Although there were some nice trails built for the archery course, Win didn't follow them. We again found ourselves along the freeway fence line heading north; with him showing some interest in the wet hollows and then nothing as we crested small rises where the wind and sun would destroy our scent clues. Winnie was getting tired. We had been out nearly three hours. We crested one more hill and below us was a father and son on the archery range shooting at hay bales but also in our general direction. My flanker called down to them so we could proceed down the hill in safety. Winnie paid no attention to the father or to the little boy. At this point Win was turning back south and I just wasn't sure of anything. We were done. We called on the radio for a ride back to the rest stop.

Upon returning, I debriefed with the OSP officer in charge. I explained the difficulties of the task again, but noted that Win did display some body language indicators that he was in scent at times. I described it as it felt like he "never locked onto a trail but instead was connecting dots — those areas where scent had pooled — heading north as least as far as the gun-club's archery range" but despite that I wasn't confident enough to run up to the local casino and put money on it." Ground searchers were deployed further north, all along the east side of the freeway.

One of the other K9 teams was also back for debriefing and her dog had alerted along Harris Creek but couldn't follow up on the scent. She asked if I would work Beryl along the same creek and see if "B" could come up with anything. She kept the location of K9 Mara's alert secret so I wouldn't be influenced and perhaps inadvertently cue my dog. I reported back that Beryl had a change of behaviour in one area but did not alert. We compared locations and they were virtually identical, but could Beryl have been "noting" the other dog's presence?

At day's end, no major discoveries were found. Two of the canines showed some interest in an area along Harris Creek but were unable to follow-up on whatever scent they had captured and Win had worked north but "it was such an old trail." We studied the terrain and wind patterns and decided the best course of action would be to search a scrub and wood covered (and tick infested) piece of land the following day just south of where Mara had alerted and Beryl had "shown interest." We also mulled over the fact that we hadn't searched the west side of the freeway although officers had done a quick check of the area where the stream re-emerged on the west side of the freeway. So, early on Wednesday K9 Beryl and K9 Mara and support personnel cleared the parcel of land.

As we worked through the scrubby parcel of land, one of my flankers called me over and said Beryl is scratching at the ground "over here." That is part of her trained final response but the not her complete response. I quickly walked over where she was standing and pawing at the bare ground. There was nothing there. Just bare ground. I had seen this behaviour the year before in the mountains above Happy Camp but it didn't seem to makes sense to me on this day. Only a short time of searching later, Beryl came racing back to me and performed her live-find alert by jumping forcefully on my legs and took my team through the dense brush. The only thing discovered, however, was a large transient camp where several people had been living. But, no sign of Elijah.

A month later, several mushroom hunters reported finding the body of a deceased adult male in an isolated wooded area about one mile northwest of the northbound Manzanita Rest Area along Interstate 5 north of Grants Pass. OSP, with the assistance of Josephine County Sheriff's Office Search and Rescue members, recovered the body positively identified as Elijah Shrewsbury, age 24.

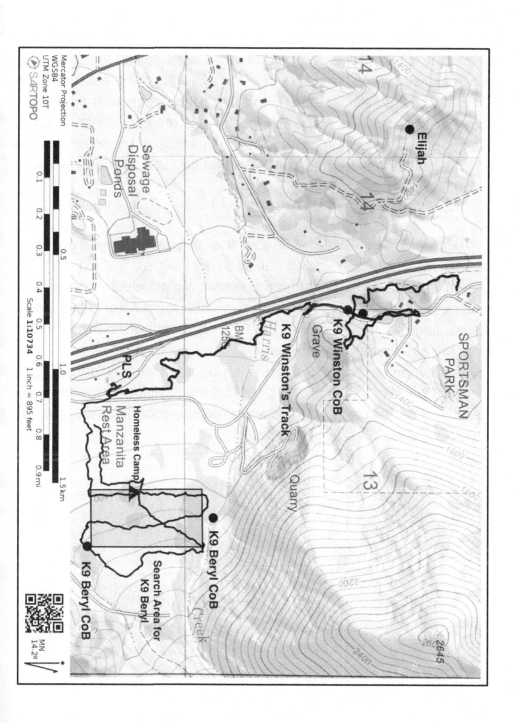

Win had been right; he had correctly determined the direction of travel. The location where Win had put his head up into the air, as if he were catching scent, was just across the freeway (due east) of where Elijah was eventually located. Prevailing wind direction in this area is from west to east. The freeway became a mental barrier to us as searchers; we were all focused on the east side of the Interstate, the side the rest stop is located on. Elijah had crossed the freeway before taking his life.

----------

A couple of months later, instead of the call coming several days after the subject had gone missing, the call came almost immediately. For several years when an endangered person (a child, elderly person, etc.) went missing in Josephine County, our SAR Coordinator called the K9 Unit as soon as they received the 911 call from our county dispatch. This proved invaluable on several searches. Any search is an emergency but especially when a child or an elderly person goes missing; time is of the essence. It also is beneficial for our canines; less contamination to sort through, less distraction, and the scent clues are generally more viable, easier to detect.

# "I'm Ruth"

**Thursday, May 26th, 2011 at 1149 pm.** "What was that?" "We need to mark this spot," Winnie pulling hard into his harness, getting tangled in the brush but still moving forward and further into the confusion of dark vegetation clawing and grabbing at us like some wicked fairy tale.

"This is Josephine County Search and Rescue, we're looking for your neighbor Ruth," Doug calls out thinking the sound we hear to be a curious neighbor.

A voice, both weak and strong and somewhat defiant of the predicament she has found herself in, calls back into the night, "I'm Ruth."

**Fifteen minutes earlier.** "Take scent Win. Find her," I whispered to my canine partner as he sniffed the gauze scent pad in the Ziplock bag. We were on the front lawn of a well-kept manufactured home on what looked, even at this late hour and through a lightly falling rain, to be a pretty tree-lined street. The gentle quiet evening broken now with the arrival of law enforcement and search and rescue vehicles, concerned neighbors walking, looking, calling-out and just hoping to spot Ruth. Flashlight beams punctuating the darkness, their beams obviously too small and narrow against the night.

Winnie immediately took me to the front door of the home and sat. "Yes, this is Ruth's house." I gave a slight tug on the lead. Win raced around to the back of the house and climbed the few stairs that led to the white-painted back door and sat. "Yes, this is Ruth's house," as I gave a slight pull on the lead. Win bounded down the stairs with urgency, his head every now and then held high indicating Ruth was possibly close-by. He led us to what appeared to be a guest house located immediately behind the home where Ruth and her husband lived; or, perhaps it was the property's original house as the older wood constructed home with its wrap around front porch conveyed a certain quaintness befitting the neighborhood. Win sat pensively at the front door and pushed at it with his nose. I reached for the door handle and a little to my surprise the door opened. It was pitch-black inside but that didn't deter Win as he raced ahead into the darkened room. Doug's flashlight illuminated a light cord hanging from the ceiling; he pulled it. Yes. The main room was now dimly lit revealing a room filled with boxes, boxes I imagined containing wonderful cherished memories from a previous younger time. Closets are filled with old clothes. Win quickly searches all the rooms, bounding around and over the boxes and even checks inside the bathtub. He leads me to a back door which I open for him but he puts the brakes on indicating "no, not this way." We then exited the way we came in, through the front door, and found ourselves on the driveway on the west side of the house; the driveway where Ruth took a walk almost each day in the company of her husband. Winnie started down the driveway to the south and toward the river swollen with spring runoff, but then slowed; his body language revealing what his nose was telling him. "Her scent is here but it's older, this isn't right." He circles behind the quaint house filled with boxes and returns to the manufactured homes white-painted back-door. All of his energy indicating that she is "right here!" "Where is she Winnie? Where?"

We make another trip through the little wooden house, this time going upstairs to check two small rooms and a closet. Then out the front door again. Win circles around toward the driveway again but instead of following it he quickly climbs the stairs to a 3rd home on the property. At the top of the stairs, he quickly turns back, "nope not here." Winnie pulls towards a wooden gate. I'm not sure where this leads but push the gate open. We are in what appears to be a more formal backyard garden; Doug helps to light the way as we cross a patch of wet lawn.

Win charges ahead, breaking through whatever scent eddy he was trapped in. He pulls us through a wood pile, I trip a bit, and then we negotiate a large pile of conifer branches and then straight into the ivy and blackberry and other thick brush before us all enclosed by the arms of a drooping cedar tree. "What was that?"

**1110 pm**. The street is dark. A lone Sheriff's Deputy with a small flashlight trying to penetrate the darkness walks along the street. I see Doug's familiar car. Doug will flank me tonight unless Ruth is found before we start. I pull to the side of the road and park on the street in front of a well-lit home. We are the first SAR personnel to arrive on scene. Two patrol cars, sit idling in the driveway of the modest manufactured home. I peer into the brightly lit windows hoping to see the deputy in charge to receive a briefing on the situation. I don't see a sole. It's so quiet. I call my SAR coordinator. Just then, the deputy walks out of the house to give me a short briefing.

*"Ruth is 92 years old. She has Alzheimer's disease. She has been missing a couple of hours now. Her husband thinks that she might have left via the back door but isn't sure. They went walking every day along the driveway on the west side of the house. She's never gone wandering before. Another deputy who has joined us reports that a neighbor found her once near their property. The deputy then whispers that the driveway leads down to the river where there is sharp drop-off into the Rogue. Another neighbor who lives along the river reported hearing her dogs barking loudly about the time Ruth went missing."*

I take in all the information at the same time trying to remember not to let it influence my thoughts about where Ruth might be. I will need to trust my dog.

But first, I will need a scent article, something of Ruth's to let Winnie know who to search for. I'm escorted into the home where Ruth's husband, clearly worried, approaches me with a shirt of his wife's but says, uncertainty entering his soft voice, "she likes to wash things." Thankfully, the deputy spoke before I needed too, "that's okay, the canine handler would like to collect her own scent article." I was escorted into the bedroom. My eyes quickly scanned the room. I saw a pair of what looked like slippers on the floor near the bathroom and asked Ruth's husband if they were hers. Did she wear them often? I then joked with him, "you don't wear them, right?" He laughed a little, some of the tension broken. I inserted a piece of 2 x 2 gauze into one of the slippers. The couple's son was there and asked a couple of questions. I briefly explained what I was doing. Time seemed to pass slowly. I always feel a bit awkward being in someone else's home; collecting a scent article seems to be so personnel, a little invasive even. I quickly bagged the gauze and headed out to my vehicle to where my canine partner was waiting.

**1020 pm.** Sound asleep except for "what is that irritating ring. What the heck." It finally registers, "Oh crap, the telephone." I lazily reach for the bedside phone to hear the familiar cheerful voice of my SAR Coordinator. We have a search.

----------

### 92-Year-Old Missing Woman Located by Search and Rescue K9

**Case #:** 2011-4733; **Incident Location:** 4600 block, Averill Dr

Grants Pass, OR — At 9:40 p.m. last night, 92-year-old Ruth H. Selle was reported missing from her home in the 4600 block of Averill Dr. Sheriff Gil Gilbertson, Undersheriff Don Fasching, Search and Rescue coordinator Sara Rubrecht, Sergeant Ray Webb, three deputies and multiple Search and Rescue volunteers responded to search for her. Neighbors were contacted and advised to keep an eye out for Selle. Sheriff's dispatchers sent out an alert to community members. Deputies checked all foot trails at the nearby park and also checked to see if Selle had been admitted at Three Rivers Community Hospital.

Three Search and Rescue K9s with their four handlers arrived on-scene and, shortly after, at 11:49 p.m., handler Ann McGloon with her K9 Winnie located Selle on a neighboring property in a patch of blackberries. Selle was not injured and did not require any medical attention. She was returned back to her family's care.

----------

Full circle. This was why Winston had come home after all. Life is like that. There is a reason for everything and this was Winston's reason. His purpose.

*High five Winnie!*

# Twin Lakes

In the early morning of May of 2021, I was sitting at the kitchen table drinking a cup of hot strong coffee and scrolling through emails, messages, and the news when a story caught my eye. A man by the name of Harry Burleigh, age 69, had been found alive after being lost in the wilderness for 17 days! The drama had occurred in the area of Twin Lakes, a remote, ruggedly beautiful area located in Douglas County, Oregon which is the county directly north of Josephine. As I read the press article, a rush of emotions and ten-year-old memories came flooding back. It was in late October, early November 2011, when I had found myself assisting in a search in this exact same area for an elk hunter of about the same age as Mr. Burleigh.

----------

Steve Litsey, 71, was from Paradise, CA. He was hunting with a friend and after a Sunday morning solo hunt, he simply vanished. Myself, K9 Winston and several other searchers from Josephine County pulled into the command area before 0800 on a very cold, very wet autumn day. It was Monday October 31st. As the day progressed, it only got colder. The area is a forested wilderness, part of the Umpqua National Forest. Just getting here took some effort. After heading north on I-5 to Roseburg, we headed east for another 60 miles with the last dozen of those miles on a gravel road winding up into the mountains, just shy of 5,000 feet in elevation. Everything seemed big here. The cliffs and drop-offs, the trees, the thick willows choking the springs and creeks, the rhododendron thickets.

The subject's camper was parked at the Twin Lakes trailhead and I was asked to start my canine from this location in an effort to determine a direction of travel or as we always wish for, to locate the missing person. It had been 48 hours since Steve had been last seen so finding a viable trail was going to be challenging, but maybe we could discover some clues.

I used a piece of 2 x 2 cotton gauze pad to collect a scent article by transferring the subject's scent from the inside of one of his plaid shirts to the cotton gauze. Steve's friend confirmed to me that the shirt hadn't been handled by anyone else. From the point-last-seen (PLS), Winston started down the main trail and worked due west adjacent to a small stream toward a spring before leaving the established trail and entering an absolutely beautiful large meadow. Winnie wound his way north hugging the tree line bordering the meadow.

As we passed one of the large conifers that overlooked the meadow, Winston stopped and sniffed all around the base of the tree and then he lifted his nose and started sniffing intently at the bark of the tree that faced into the meadow below. In that moment I mused how peculiar that was until my support noted what a magnificent place it would be to sit and overlook the meadow and watch the elk move in and out of the shadows.

Winston began circling the area and then just a short distance from the curious tree, his behaviour changed as he began to air scent lifting his nose directly into the wind. Wind direction at the time was from the north northeast at a bearing of roughly 60 degrees. I tried to capture that fleeting moment when the dog first catches the scent and instinctively faces directly into the wind. When taking a bearing, I give myself a little wiggle room, between 5 and 10 degrees to take into account the terrain and the angle I am at when the dog faces into the wind. Winston crested a ridge and we intersected the main Twin Lakes trail, where Winnie's behaviour changed again; he lost the scent he just had.

Shortly, thereafter, we came upon a trail junction. A half-eaten banana lay by the trail probably discarded by a fellow searcher. Winston, who was quite adept at multi-tasking when food was involved, grabbed the banana and just kept on working. He was a funny little dog. At about this time we received a radio call asking us to check a footprint located west of a spring. I was excited that a potential physical clue had been discovered and we immediately headed back to the spring. Unfortunately, Winston could not pick up a direction of travel from the area where the footprint was located.

I recall taking a break at this spring. It was cold and rainy. I wrapped Winston up in a coat to keep him warm while we organized our thoughts and conferred with a canine air scent team from Douglas County that was working in the area. We decided to search along the trail that headed south and then due west to the 530 road. This trail winds its way 1,000 feet above the Twin Lakes and on the flanks of the mountain with the same name. As Winston worked and we took in the amazing expansive views, Win showed another significant change of behaviour. He turned his body into the cliffside and tried to climb through the jumble of rocks upward, chasing scent as it wafted higher and higher. At the time there was a strong updraft coming directly up the cliff face. We marked the area on our GPS and called the information back into command.

It had been a long cold tiring day. We had started our search at 0830 that morning and didn't return to base until 1530 in the afternoon. We huddled in the yurt that had been set up as a debriefing area equipped with hot coffee and snacks. In my debrief report, I suggested further search efforts should be conducted where Winston's first change of behaviour had fizzled (I drew a black box on a map for operations planners) and also the east side of the larger lake which was directly

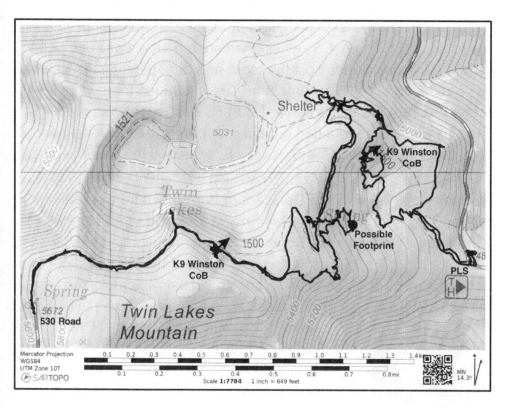

below the cliff face that Winston tried so hard to climb as the winds were drawn higher.

Arriving home well into the early evening, it was time for reflection, a hot shower and a proper meal. The following day was spent at home resting and pouring over maps, trying to figure out what, if anything, Winnie had smelled out there on the trail.

When the phone rang that evening asking if I could go back, the answer was a resounding yes. I would this time bring K9 Beryl as my teammate. Denise would bring K9 Cody and then seven ground searchers from Josephine County would round out the compliment of those getting up before dawn to make the long drive back to the search area. It was now Wednesday November 2nd.

Our first search assignment was unusual. We were all assigned to one team, JoCo Team 4. The assigned search area was quite large so we made the decision to split the team and our search area in two. As the canine handler, I became the Team Leader for searching the northern part of the search area; Doug H. was my trusted support and Brian O., and Joe L. rounded out our four person team. Denise and K9 Cody, Kate O., Dan G., Joe S., Lucky B. searched the south segment.

The plan was we to grid search as best we could from north to south and then meet up with the Denise and her team who were searching from south to the north. K9 Beryl, myself and Doug H. searched the steep draw leading into the Copeland Creek drainage and then worked

south while Joe and Brian paralleled our route of travel but stayed below some of the steeper rock faces. The entire team was thwarted by sheer drop offs and extremely steep and hazardous terrain that prevailed in the search area. Much of the southern portion of the search area was not covered due to extreme terrain.

Having a small dog came in handy as we carefully negotiated the terrain. There was one spot where we tip toed along a small shelf along a rocky cliff face that Doug thought it would be safer if we carried Beryl across the precarious slope. He lifted her up and she happy went for a short safe ride in his arms.

*Doug ensuring K9 Beryl gets across the cliff face safely*

Due to the hazardous terrain and no clues being found, we were back doing our debrief by 1300 hours.

There was plenty of daylight left so we were given another assignment. We were asked to search two areas more thoroughly; first, the "spring draw," which was an area where air scent dogs had shown

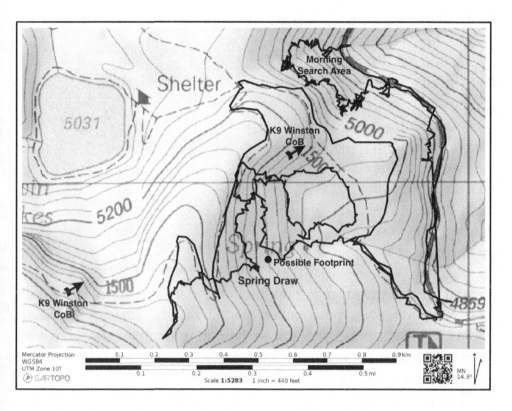

some interest and secondly the west side of the meadow where Winston, two days prior, lifted his head trying to capture the scent floating on the wind. We made a quick turnaround at base and we were back on the hunt by 1330.

With Doug along as my support, we worked "little B" up the draw and like the other air scent dogs, she became quite animated but never gave me a formal indication. We then continued to search the treeline between the meadow and the forest and up toward the ridge to the west. The trees were so big and Beryl looked so small as she bounded through the grasses hunting the wind. As we concluded our search of this area, JoCo K9 2 (Denise with K9 Cody supported by Lucky) requested we rendevous with them at their location. Denise reported that Cody had given her two strong alerts in the area. We conferred and wind direction at the time was from the west to the east directly down the draw. We decided to work up the draw as far as the first

*Doug confirming our position within the meadow*

plateau area. As we climbed up through the thick willows of the draw, Denise reporting two more canine alerts by Cody. This ridge area and the associated spring fed draws figured predominately in several reports by canine handlers including my very own Winston. As we reached the plateau we were met with a wall of rhododendrons. I had Beryl search the area – one of her forte's was getting into and through the thickest of vegetation - but we came up empty. We were running out of light and there was still more area to cover. If only our dogs could talk; actually, they do talk, the question is are we listening. Of course, when we returned to base at 5 pm after another long day, we suggested further search efforts be conducted in this area.

But heavy snow began to fall that Wednesday night, so much snow that the search was halted for the season. Steve Litsey has never been found.

----------

I always wanted to return to this area but the opportunity never arose. I believe Douglas County searchers returned at a later time to revisit

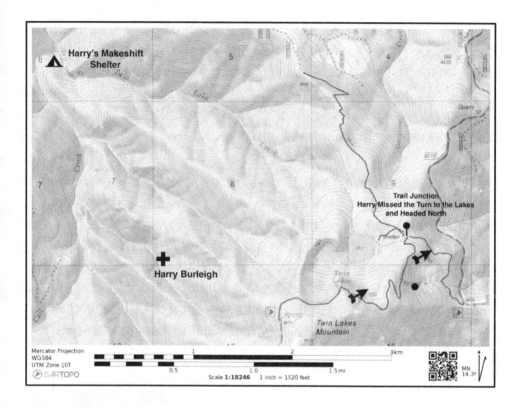

and hopefully find some clues or maybe even Steve. As I sat at the kitchen table reading the incredible story of Harry Burleigh and how he had missed a simple turn in the trail and had gotten sucked into one of the rugged creek drainages. I pulled out my old search maps and studied them one more time and I wondered if Mr. Litsey could have befallen a similar fate. Harry recounts how he missed the sharp left hand turn toward the Lakes and instead headed northwest away from the lake and along a ridge dividing the Twin Lake Creek and Deception Creek drainages. This is the same trail intersection where Winston found the discarded banana. What if it had belonged to Steve? I didn't have an article indication on my canine. This would be an easy intersection to get turned around at; turning left or north leads downhill and to get back to the trailhead you need to go downhill as well, just in the opposite direction. The terrain kept pulling Mr. Burleigh further away from the lakes and he found himself at the confluence of Twin Lake and Calf Creek where he set up a makeshift shelter. After spending several days here, he decided to move up a nearby unnamed creek drainage which he believed would lead him back to the Twin Lakes. It was along this creek drainage that he was finally found by search and rescue personnel.

It's never easy when a search doesn't reach some sort of conclusion. For the family it is of course, heart breaking. The legal ramifications for the family can also be a bit of a nightmare. Without a body, death insurance lags behind leaving the grieving family with more stress and uncertainty. It wasn't until 2013 that Steve Litsey was legally pronounced deceased by the Douglas County District Court. For us searchers, it's that feeling that perhaps if we had looked behind just one more tree or bush or rock outcropping, if we had followed the dog just a little bit further, we might have found a clue. Or better yet, brought the missing home.

*Close of day, Twin Lakes, Oregon*

# Clues Come in Many Forms

CORSAR callouts were responsible for most of the searches I was involved in for some reason, and I found myself in Siskiyou County, CA a lot. And the area around the small town of Etna in particular.

It was the beginning of the second week of May 2012 that we were called to look for Mr. James Hardaway, an elderly man suffering from Alzheimer's disease. My good friend Lynda was to flank for Winnie and me. We arrived late on a Tuesday morning and Mr. Hardaway had been missing since early evening the night before. It was going to be a hot day, near 90 degrees, and we were going to get a late start and be working during some of the worst hours of the day.

Mr. Hardaway had walked away from him home. To the west were large hay fields and to the east the fields gave way to pine forested hills. A meandering creek, Miners Creek, with its share of blackberries along the banks, divided the fields from the forest while irrigation ditches, full at this time of the year, lined the lush fields. Command and all the paraphernalia that comes along with it had set up just outside the back door to the residence. After explaining a bit how a trailing dog works, I was escorted by a Siskiyou County Sheriff's Deputy into the house to collect a scent article.

Collecting a good quality scent article can make for a successful trail or one that ends at the wrong person or never even gets started. When possible, I liked to use actual items that belonged to the missing person but that isn't always possible. For this search I used a 2 x 2 gauze pad to transfer scent from the armpit area of two recently worn shirts. I double-upped or overdid it by also collecting scent from the foot area found under the sheets at the bottom of his side of the bed. I had been briefed that Mrs. Hardaway had last seen her husband departing the residence by the door that existed into the backyard and a patio area. She recalled seeing him then take a familiar path from the backyard through an open section of fence and that was the last she saw of him. My plan was then to start Winnie in the backyard after first letting Winston sniff Mrs. Hardaway and eliminate her as who we were searching for.

K9 Winston initially headed south from the house before circling north and then back to the residence eliminating directions of travel during the wide circle. Once back at residence, he started again but this time with much more confidence. We headed again south, through the search base area which had set-up pretty much on top of the point-last-seen, and then Winston crossed the road, and through a broken wooden gate mostly blocked by SAR vehicles and up a small gravel driveway. A discarded apple, yup he picked it up, gave it a few good chomps and without missing a beat kept pulling us along the driveway. As we approached a double-wide mobile home, Winston's behaviour changed dramatically. A scent pool proximity alert! There was a steep 20-foot drop-off above Miners Creek. Winston frenetically circled the area before breaking out of the scent pool and heading south along a small dirt path. After about 500 feet though he turned back around toward the mobile home. The scent pool was playing tricks on him; since south was his initial direction of travel out of the scent pool, I suggested to him that perhaps we check down along the creek. Winston thought that was an okay idea and he crossed to the west bank of the creek then after about 500 feet, he wasn't sure anymore. At this point, it was approximately 1300 hours on a hot afternoon, we were asked to return-to-base. We hadn't exhausted our options but something must be up to call us back.

A clue had been found! A comb and blue cup had been located and verified as belonging to Mr. Hardaway. It was just a bit further south from the mobile home than we travelled. We were quickly escorted to the clue's location. I scented Winston and we began our search again.

Winston took us south along Miners Creek, crossing it back and forth a few times, but it never felt quiet right and the further south we progressed the less confident we both got. We emerged from the creek bed at Sugar Creek Road where Winston completely had lost the plot. With nothing to follow, we opted to return to base. It was now 1515 hours in the afternoon.

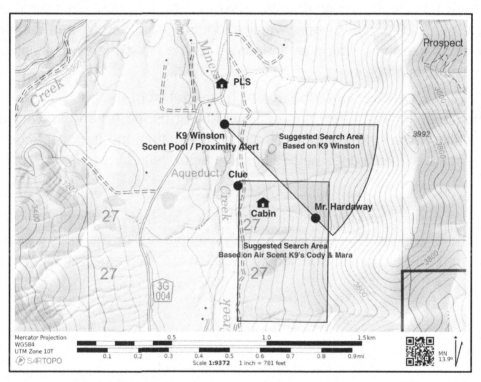

After returning to base and being debriefed, the Josephine County canine handlers all got together and started plotting our tracks and our scent clues on Monica's computer. I had strongly suggested in my formal debrief that the "hillside to the east of where Winston gave his scent pool-proximity alert be thoroughly searched." In reviewing the terrain, I noted that it was possible that Mr. Hardaway was above the creek to the east, his scent pooling in the creek bed overnight which is consistent with normal diurnal wind flow. I indicated during that debrief that these scent pools, based on terrain and experience, can be as far as ¼ - ½ mile from the subject. The air scent handlers, Monica and Denise, reported that their dogs kept pulling them to the north and up the hill (they had been searching the hillside to the south near Sugar Creek road). After all of our data was plotted onto the computer's mapping system, we briefed the Siskiyou County Deputy in charge of the search. As part of her investigation, she had learned and shared with us that there was a cabin located up the hill in the exact location we suggested be searched.

As we headed home that evening, we got word that Mr. Hardaway had been located a few hundred feet further up the hill and above the cabin. Those long distance "alerts" from Winston and the scent clues from the air scent dogs helped to solve a puzzle in May.

---

At the end of May I found myself back in Siskiyou County for yet another search. This one was full of adventure testing the skills we had honed over the years, from land navigation to the unexpected night out.

# Handler Skills

In addition to be on the K9 Unit, I took the required courses to become a Search Manager (and assisted on a few searches over the years) but what I really enjoyed was teaching the necessary foundational skills that searchers need in order to be competent while out in the field. Two of my favorite topics were land navigation – where I stressed map and compass skills over becoming reliant on a GPS – and search tactics.

I have always loved maps. I suspect my love for maps grew out of traveling through much of Europe during summertime family vacations when I was young. My mom, who was the premier planner for our driving adventures on the Continent, always had a love for the smaller road lines on the map, and whoever was gifted with the passenger seat for the day was responsible for keeping us on mom's planned route. I loved being chosen to be the days navigator and unfolding the Michelin map across my lap and following our route with my finger. I definitely inherited that love of the backroads; just ask my husband who raises his eyebrows every time I plan a drive. In college I studied and graduated in Geography and after graduation I went to Washington D.C. to start a US Government career in the intelligence field where for near twenty-years maps, satellite imagery and ground photography became the back bone of everything I became involved in.

While employed with the government, I learned even more about maps (those big white uncharted areas always the most intriguing in my mind), different coordinate systems, ground truthing, and calling a halt when things aren't going quite as planned. One story I like to recount took place in Laos. My team and I had travelled to Laos to conduct an opium poppy ground truth survey. We arrived with our satchel of maps and coordinates that we would share with our helicopter pilots so they could fly us to specific locations in the remote mountains. We were there

to ground-truth, to ensure that what we categorized as opium poppy fields from satellite imagery were in fact poppy fields. Through US Embassy contacts, I rented an MI-17 helicopter which unfortunately limited access to some areas because of its large size. After briefing the pilots as best we could, we took off and it became evident fairly quickly that the maps and coordinates we brought with us did not correspond with the maps and coordinate systems they were using. The helicopter landed in a grassy field; we got out, laid down the maps and compared the two different versions, studied the odd Russian symbols and then replotted all of our data. Lesson learned.

----------

I guess it was no surprise then that on my very first search as a ground searcher, I raised my hand as we were about to enter the field as I suspected our initial direction of travel was incorrect and we were going to be searching the wrong area.

That first search was in a place called Emily Creek, an incredibly steep and thickly wooded area in Curry County, Oregon. It was, however, a great place to hunt for mushrooms and each year during the season it drew seasonal mushroom hunters to comb the forest floor. Ironically, the Emily Creek drainage was not only my first search but it was an area I revisited as my time with SAR drew to a close. That first search took place in the fall of 2005, a Vietnamese man who's name I can no longer remember had become separated from his family group while hunting mushrooms. I was assigned to a ground team and we were ferried via all-terrain-vehicle (ATV) to the end of an old logging road where we were to commence our search. From the end of the logging-road we were given a compass bearing and it would be along that heading that would define that day's search efforts. Our Team Leader looked at the map and saw the end of the road clearly depicted and based on that pointed to the direction we were to search. I, however, had plopped my map on the ground and taken out my compass to double check our direction of travel. I wanted to be absolutely sure I knew where I was before I stepped off the safety of the road and into the bush. Things were just not jiving. I tentatively spoke up holding my compass in the air "Are you sure, my compass is showing me something different?" She took her own compass out and her map and then saw her mistake. She assumed the road we were standing on had been correctly depicted on the map and it had not. We headed off in the "new" correct direction. In a weird twist of fate, if we had searched along the incorrect heading, we might have found the lost man that very day. He was discovered the next day directly on what would have been our route of travel. Sadly, he was deceased.

----------

Fast forward to 2017. After a full day of hasty searching (by ground searchers and our now infamous local pilot John Rachor) for an overdue hiker in the Kalmiopsis Wilderness, I was asked to plot and devise a search plan for the US Coast Guard and then fly with the crew to conduct an aerial search. My first plan of action was to talk to some experts about the trails in the Kalmiopsis and so I reached out to Gabriel Howe, Executive Director and Founder of the Siskiyou Mountain Club, for on the ground knowledge of the area. That evening I bounced some flight ideas of my husband, a pilot who spent most of his flight career searching for Soviet submarines or South American drug runners from the flight deck of a P-3, and then I put together a plan. I absolutely loved this type of planning. I had mapped clandestine airfields throughout northern Mexico, helped put together targeting packages for cocaine laboratory raids in South America, and had mapped illicit crop growing areas around the world. Now I might get to use these same mapping and planning skills to help save a life. The Siskiyou Mountain Club penned an article on the resulting rescue.

*"On Friday, June 9, Matt Denberg set out to backpack the Leach Memorial Loop in three days. The 48-mile route traverses the rugged Kalmiopsis Wilderness, a place known for its rugged and unforgiving terrain. He forded the Chetco River on Bailey Mountain Trail 1109. Then it started to rain.*

*Chetco River location where Matt was rescued*

*And it kept raining.*

*Then he hopped onto Upper Chetco Trail 1102, contouring westward along the Chetco's rugged banks, and climbed up and over a ridge to Box Canyon Creek. But the raging tributary was too high to ford, and he'd later tell Josephine County Search and Rescue volunteer Ann McGloon that he almost drowned there.*

*"I think he got a scare from that," she says.*

*So, he headed back the way he came, towards Babyfoot, okay with cutting his trip early with an out and back. But by then, the Chetco was too high to ford safely.*

*Monday afternoon came, and Matt's friends grew worried. By Tuesday, June 15, Josephine County Search and Rescue had planes searching for Denberg along the Leach Memorial Loop.*

*Denberg had heard the planes, and tried to wave them down with his orange bag. "Because of the canyon, they could not see him," McGloon says.*

By Wednesday, the US Coast Guard had mobilized and McGloon was flying along Denberg's planned route, which she was somewhat familiar with. She took the helicopter toward Bailey Mountain, and from there down to the Chetco.

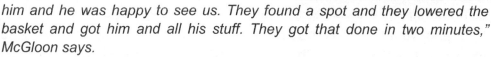

"We had him in seven minutes," she says. "He was waving a white piece of Tyvek," she says.

Then pilots let down a 300-foot rope with a radio for Denberg to confirm his identity and that he needed help.

"These guys were amazing. The helicopter didn't move. We confirmed it was him and he was happy to see us. They found a spot and they lowered the basket and got him and all his stuff. They got that done in two minutes," McGloon says.

"He was in good spirits," McGloon adds. She emphasizes using a good signal when trying to get found. "A cell phone. The flash of your camera. You don't think of that stuff when you're stressed."

With unseasonably high streams, and the potential of marine storms to bring them even higher, hikers and backpackers need to take careful diligence in planning ahead. "He was testing the water level with a stick; it didn't go down much" McGloon said."

----------

Searching and navigating at night adds another layer of complexity to any search, even those that seem fairly straight forward. In November of 2010 SAR was activated to search for a couple of young adults who had been out hunting for mushrooms and were now overdue. This time, however, we were much closer to home and in significantly less daunting terrain. It was the middle of the night when one of the ATV teams heard the young men shouting from the darkness beyond the mud track. One three-person K9 team (Randy with K9 Josie, Ruth, and Joe) and one ground team were deployed to where the ATV team heard the calls for help and we headed up in what was expected to be a quick search conclusion. Monica and I comprised the two-person ground team; prior to our trek up the slope, we took a quick bearing on the direction that it seemed the voices were coming from, approximately 275 degrees, or due west. Simple. As we ventured up and into the dark woods, we immediately noticed an old skid-road heading in mostly the correct direction. As we climbed higher, the voices got louder, higher up still and now directly in front and west of us. We had no choice but to leave the overgrown skid road and bush whack at this point. The voices were closer still. They were responding to our calls. How easy was this night turning out to be. As we dropped down into a drainage, however, silence. The drainage was exceedingly steep and we had to carefully and slowly find footholds and handholds to descend. At this point we noticed the K9 team was above us, further up the drainage. Radio contact confirmed that they had found an "easier" crossing point. We locked on to the shine of their headlamps and finally met up with them. As the combined teams now climbed out of the drainage, we started hearing the voices again. Above us still, to the west, no wait, below us; while sound does carry exceedingly well at night, the local terrain was playing havoc as their cries of "over here," echoed all around us. They had noticed the same thing and discovered by actually lowering their voices and by more calmly calling instead of yelling, they heard less echo and so did we. We continued up and west. Joe kept them talking to us so we could "walk toward the sound." So close now and yet another small drainage!

And this one was really steep. They were on the other side, their little pocket light fading but pointing the way for us. The last climb, up a 70 degree plus muddy slope about 100 feet to the two young men waiting for rescue. Since leaving the ATV's, it has taken an hour to hone in on their voices; we had travelled a mere 1/3 of a mile and climbed about 400 feet.

The two young men, other than a bit cold — it was a chilly 35-degree night — were in good condition and had done everything right. Most importantly, they had stayed in place. They had a cell phone with them that provided an important "ping," to help the first on scene narrow down the search area (their vehicle was a good half-mile down the road). They used some of their extra plastic bags that they had brought to carry their collected mushrooms in and placed them over their socks to keep their feet dry. After providing them with some warmer clothes, they were fit to walk out of the woods.

Walking back out, however, wasn't much easier than the trek in. We attempted to try and keep away from the worst of the terrain which then posed a bit of a navigational challenge. It meant deviating from the "go-to" GPS prompt which wasn't too useful anyway as our rate of travel was too slow. Although the paper map we had that night was lacking in detail, it was those unfashionable, but critically important, map and compass skills that proved to be the best navigational tool. As we rested on top of a rocky slope, I pulled out the map, plotted our UTM position, got a compass direction from our position to the ATV's, took a bearing and we headed out. And like magic, after only a few feet, an old skid road appeared. We hadn't seen in it initially even though we had been sitting practically on top of it during our rest break; and, it was fortuitously heading exactly on our desired bearing of 130 degrees. As we got further down the slope, Monica and I recognized it as the road we had initially walked up. An hour later, we were all safely back at the ATV's.

Searching at night, a required SAR skill, poses some unique challenges. Your headlamp or flashlight only shines so far limiting your field of view and your ability to orient yourself to the terrain around you. Time and distance are more difficult to gauge. Hazards are not visible until you are directly on top of them; clues that a drastic terrain change is approaching are not as easily discernible. And avenues of travel (like old skid roads or game trails) can be invisible to you and yet only a few feet away. Navigation is just much harder. There are other night time skills that are equally as important and one of those is just being comfortable spending that unexpected night out. So, we train for that too.

----------

It was April of 2011 and our annual Search and Rescue Academy was coming to its grand finale, testing gear by spending a night in the woods after a full day of searching because the days do really turn into nights. This year I brought K9 Winston along for the training as well.

"Settle down, Winnie, settle please." Thud, he drops like one of the heavy stones that pepper the soil that lie underneath our camp site forcing our bodies into contorted positions to find any comfort. We go through this drill in what seems like a hundred times throughout the wet night. You see Win has appointed himself guardian of our two-team campsite along Mendenhall Creek; and, rather than curl up against my body to keep me warm like all those dogs do in the movies he watches and listens pensively to the forest sounds all night. Every now and then a searcher awakens to stoke the fire or make a trip into the woods for some personal business and that usually solicits a throaty WOOF from Win. "That's a good boy Win, scare the cougars away," shouts Bill from his tarp-draped shelter. "It's just Monica," I whisper to my brown dog. "Go to sleep." God, this is going to be a long night.

After a full day of training, this night spent in the woods was the final "test" for new SAR recruits. The day started out like most days for the past month and a half, cloudy, drizzly, with rain showers expected. The mineral rich clay soils were saturated and water was running off the mountain slopes pooling anywhere flat forming swampy bogs. The warm wet weather melted snow at higher elevations and creeks were running full.

Being a K9 handler does have its advantages, I was given permission to drive my personal vehicle to our training location while virtually all others rode in the worn olive-green "Blue-Bird" bus ably driven by the County Sheriff. As soon as the bus riders arrived, training began. The day's training focused on search tactics culminating in a mock-search exercise. Eight teams were formed to search individual designated areas for a presumably responsive subject. Most teams found their "lost subject," within 20 minutes but quickly learned that a probable unresponsive subject may also be within their search areas. Teams began finding their unresponsive subjects, the newspaper stuffed dummies had suffered more than a good soaking. The scenarios played out and each team learned that their faux subject, was the victim of a crime. Teams were transitioning from the various types of searches to securing crime-scenes using the protocols they learned during week one of training. The entire time it was raining. As a team leader, I was impressed with the caliber of the new recruits. Everyone took turns on the radio and acting as Team Leader. No one complained about the weather, everyone was eager to learn. Team 4 rocked!

I had brought K9 Winston with me to spend the night out. I'd taken him camping in my home-built teardrop trailer before, but wasn't sure if he'd ever just slept out in the elements before. This was a skill I wanted him to have, in case the occasion ever arose. I had no way of predicting that in a year, our skills would be put to the test. After spending most of the day waiting for me in the car, he was more than eager to start hiking up the muddy track to where we had planned to spend the night. He walked with enthusiasm, nose to the ground, "oh, all these people I haven't met yet have hiked up this trail, maybe they will all give me a cookie." Before any cookies were doled out, we first had to cross the creek. Two logs were laid side-by-side across the rushing water and a rope had been secured to a couple of trees to use as a hand-hold. Win confidently stepped onto the logs and crossed the creek like he had been doing this all his life. Such a good dog. And more foreshadowing of events to come.

After a short lesson on shelter making and fire starting, each team began the process of setting up their shelters to keep them dry for the night. It was still raining. Resources were pooled and the largest tarps were used for constructing a weatherproof shelter while the smaller ones were used as ground covers. In no time, a good-sized fire was going and everyone was going about the business of cooking dinner. Hot oatmeal topped with trail mix for me; Win giving me the jowl-smack of approval as I gave him a bite.

*Settling in for the night*

We all survived the damp Oregon night. Win kept all the forest animals at bay and kept me awake most of the night. Have you ever noticed how long the night can be while huddled under a tarp on a dark wet night? I would find out again, this time for real, the following year.

# An Unexpected Night Out

May 2012. It all started out quite normally. A call went out about a search in Siskiyou County, California. K9 Unit members called each other to see who was available and on this day Josephine County would be sending Monica and her air scent dog Mara and then myself and my dogs Beryl (air scent) and Winston (trailing). Two more SAR members were available to serve as flankers and we had a dedicated driver to get us there and back safely. And, off we went.

We arrived at base, the Green Valley Store along Highway 3 in the beautiful Scott Valley, just past noon. Teams were briefed. A lost hiker, 57-year-old Spence Palmer who set out for a day hike along the Pacific Crest Trail (PCT) from Mt. Etna to Kidder Creek. The hiker had been due to finish his day hike Saturday afternoon but today was Monday. A search team had located his footprints along the PCT as they left the trail to try and avoid a snow field that was blocking the way.

As we received our assignments, I knew that this day, this search, was going to be different from most. I was asked to deploy with my trailing dog from the last-known-point (LKP) and to try and determine a direction of travel of the lost hiker or locate any further clues. As we left base, I instinctively grabbed one of those infamous SAR sack lunches, often put together with prison help, and stuffed it in my 24-hour pack. My flanker Bill, K9 Winston and I were then driven to the Mt. Etna trailhead about 12 miles further up the road; a team that had already been in the field over 24 hours was there awaiting a ride back to base. As we exited the vehicle, we were hit by the wind, gusting probably 30 mph. I stuffed an extra wool cap in my pack while Bill grabbed a heavier jacket. I said goodbye to Beryl who sat in her crate in the back of the vehicle, and waited for the California Highway Patrol helicopter to land on the road and ferry us to the LKP.

I've flown in helicopters before — mostly in the jungles and mountains of South America during my time serving as an intelligence officer — but this was my first ride with my canine partner by my side. He jumped in, took his place between myself and Bill and looked out the front window like he had flown over the Marble Mountains all his life. Bill took a few pictures. The pilot added power as we passed over the ridgeline and were met with a downdraft; the pilot then expertly turned the helicopter into the strong gusting wind and gently set us down on a narrow ridgeline at 6,700 feet. We were safely out and the helicopter gone in less than a minute. As we surveyed our surroundings, a scree slope dropping precipitously to the west with snow covered slopes falling away sharply to the east, I knew we were in for a tough search and, that more than likely, we would be spending the night "out there" and not in our own beds. It was now 1400 hours.

*Looking south from the LKP into the headwaters of Big Creek*

A lone man sat under a tree. We went to check-in and he introduced himself and said he was communications relay for teams being ferried into the area. He looked at Winston and asked, "Is he a Clumber Spaniel?"

"Nope, a Sussex spaniel," I explained. "I love spaniels," he said smiling. I don't remember his name but instantly I liked him.

After introductions, I walked Win to the LKP and asked him to take scent from the scent article I had collected earlier, and then whispered

176

into his bog floppy ears "find'em." Win worked along the scree slope heading northwest and then slowly pulled us into the Big Creek drainage. He quartered methodically back and forth across the now tree covered slope; he wasn't working a trail but rather a wide and faint scent cone not directly connected to "source." As we dropped down below a rock face and reached a flattish vine maple-choked section of the North Fork of Big Creek, his pace quickened and his body language changed; he encountered a small scent pool. He raised his head and worked the wind, blowing hard now from the west. He looked across the creek several times, but the slope on the other side was snow covered and near vertical. We weren't crossing the creek. At about this time it started to sleet with a mix of snow and then finally it changed to all rain. Winston showed no other scent interest beyond this point. It was now 1600 hrs.

I learned there were two teams ahead of us further down the drainage, an air scent canine team and the communication relay team that had decided since the helicopter was now grounded due to weather, they would walk out via the Big Creek drainage. We had two options, go back up to the PCT or continue to go down and since there is something comforting in knowing others are in the same area, we chose to head downhill and walk out as well. Maybe we could link up?

As we started down the drainage it quickly became clear that "merely walking out" wasn't going to be so simple. We moved cautiously as the slopes became steeper, thick brush anchored the slippery shale in some places, but in many places the slopes were just a jumble of loose rock; one of those rock filled gullies reached almost all the way back to the ridgeline. We looked at our GPS and realized we had only gone one mile in four hours but had dropped near 2,000 feet in elevation. If I remember my high school algebra correctly (S=Rise/Run) that would be about a 38% grade. The slopes we were traversing, however, were near 50% grade. A tricky balancing act for two tired searchers and one search dog. So, at 2000 hours we decided we needed to stop. We could see the campfire of the teams ahead of us further down the draw but we knew we couldn't reach them before dark.

We put our overnight survival training to the test: collected a large pile of fire wood, built a shelter using our tarps (thankfully it had stopped raining), and settled in for the night. I owe a lot to Bill for really taking charge of the fire and despite our rocky, brushy thicket perched above a raging creek, we did have the warmth of a roaring fire and that is something really nice. I had the better trioxane fuel so I boiled us water for hot coffee and tea, another comfort that is seemingly a small thing but does amazing things for the spirit. We attempted to dry socks and other gear. Winston and I shared the prison packed bagged lunch. Didn't matter that the sandwich was soggy, we both agreed it tasted great. Winston also had some kibble that I always carry in my pack. He was tired and alternated between sitting by the fire with us and lying down in the nice hole he dug under a nearby bush. At some point we signed off the radio to save batteries; another comfort was having such a cheerful voice on the other end of the radio and knowing that there was someone there if we needed them and that they knew where we were and that my teammates back at base were looking after Beryl. At just past midnight we were tired enough that we thought we might be able to sleep. Coincidently we both had a similar bivy sac (from *Adventure Medical*) and with all my clothes on, a fleece cap and neck warmer, I crawled into my survival bivy. Winston snuggled up as close as he could but he still shivered most of the night. He also dreamed and I felt his dreams through his twitching body several times and wondered what he was dreaming about.

The fire flickered to life at 0430 and I got up — not that I had ever really slept, more liked dozed — and joined Bill at the fire. As we watched the dark sky lighten with the emerging dawn, we both knew that at some point we had crossed an invisible divide and we were no longer in search-mode but we were in survival-mode. I drank a hot cup of cocoa, ate a hard-boiled egg (part of the sack lunch), shared some potato chips with Win and then fed Win his breakfast of kibble. According to the map, we still had about 2 miles to go before we would reach the North Fork of the Salmon River where we would be rewarded with a well-travelled trail. It would take us over 6 hours!

The first challenge we had to tackle was crossing the North Fork of Big Creek. The creek was flush with snowmelt and the current was extremely strong. The creek cascaded down the mountain slope, lined by large boulders and steep sides. Bill had just taken a swift water rescue course and that gave me some comfort. After the exertion of the previous day and little sleep, our legs felt wobbly on this morning as we picked or way carefully down to the creek. Bill crossed first by taking one giant step from one large boulder to another; packs were then then handed across the creek with each of us standing on boulders, feet spread wide for balance. The current was too strong for Win to swim across and it was too awkward to safely balance on the rocks and hand him across the creek. We couldn't just pull him across; he looked a little nervous and I wasn't sure he wouldn't slip his harness. So, out of options, I tossed the end of his long line to Bill, picked Win up and with all my strength tossed him across the swiftest part of the current and Bill reeled him in like a big brown fish before he was carried away and swept over the small waterfall just below. I sat down on the boulder and shook a little bit and shed an emotional tear. I was responsible for him; he trusted me and I had just had to throw my best buddy into a cold unforgiving stream in the middle of nowhere. Deep breath.

Win shook off the cold water and looked back at me waiting for me to cross. I stood on that boulder a long time before taking the "giant step-small-leap" to get across safely. That creek crossing drained me while at the same time energized me. I was ready for this little adventure to be over. Safely on the other side, we pulled our way up the steep muddy bank and into thick brush and heavy deadfall. Not a game trail to be found. This was the one area where Winston decided to show-off his stubborn side, which ironically makes him a good trailing dog. Winston was very useful for keeping us on track; after we made our decision to "follow" the teams ahead of us down the draw the day before, Winston took that new task to heart and he trailed the teams doing a fair share of the navigating for us. But we had now crossed the creek not where the other teams had and Win had no scent to follow and was not pleased with the path we chose. I admit, it was pretty awful. After about one-quarter mile and two hours of fighting our way through the brush, we cut the other teams trail and all was well again in Winnie's mind. We next found ourselves above the confluence of the North Fork and the South Fork of Big Creek.

This creek crossing wasn't as terrifying, maybe because we were both now extremely tired. We just did it. Bill crossed first, packs handed across, Winnie tossed into the swift current and reeled to shore, I cross. Packs back on. One foot in front of the other. The forest opened up a bit and we did manage to locate a faint game trail and Winston confirmed we were following the correct route. After four more hours we made it to the Salmon River and the trail back to Mule Bridge. We hiked the last 5 miles along the trail in about 2 hours, admiring the crystal-clear North Fork Salmon River as we walked. The sight of the old green steel and wooden bridge and SAR personnel brought the biggest smile to my face! We were out, had done it, and we got news that our missing hiker had been found alive just moments earlier.

We were driven down the road to a clearing where a Blackhawk helicopter waited. We were air lifted back across the mountains we had just descended and back to base. Winnie lied down between the seats and promptly fell asleep bringing a warm smile to the Army sergeant's face who was manning the door. Upon exiting the aircraft, we saw Monica and Lynda standing there smiling and waving. Lots of hugs all around. Lynda took Winston, Monica my pack, another canine handler offered lemonade, a third enquired if I needed dog food for Winnie. Nope, he was having one (or maybe two) of the chicken burritos being made up by the Siskiyou chaplain who was manning the improvised kitchen. It felt so good to be "out." Skills put to the test; not a training exercise but the real thing and we had done good.

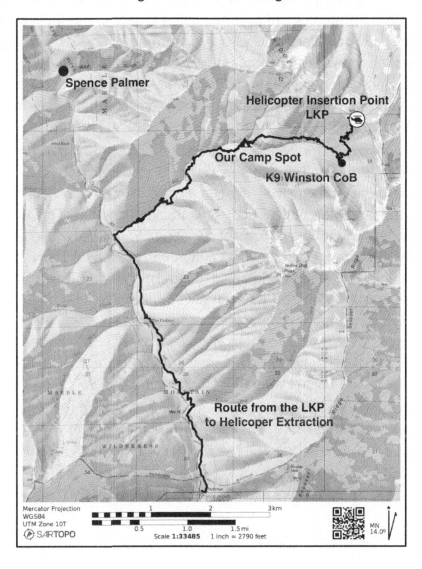

—————————

After the emotional highs of some excellent searches, things began to change within our tight-knit K9 Unit and over the summer that cohesiveness started to fray a bit at the seams. Even to this day I am not sure completely why but as Unit Leader, I shoulder some of the responsibility regardless of the underlying reasons. A couple handlers departed, new handlers arrived, there were new puppies in the group, we had a change of SAR coordinators, just so many things going on all at once. Some friendships started to unravel like a string of cloth caught on a tree branch and then cast upon the wind. Tensions were in the air all fall and seemed to only increase as time progressed.

It was also time for Winnie to recertify. I had to head over to Sisters to recertify Beryl in HRD that summer so why not give Winnie's OSSA trailing evaluation a go. Well, despite a good start he missed a turn and we got too far off the trail to recover. Coming on the heels of such good solid trailing work, it was rather disappointing. We would need to recertify so I arranged for another test in early fall to take advantage of some cooler weather. Another testing opportunity arose in early September but he missed a turn near the start this time and although he worked hard to recover and tried to get back to it, he couldn't and we failed again. Was it time to retire Winnie? Winnie seemed tired and we went for a vet check; he was a bit anemic. I let him rest. In reviewing my logbook, I notice I didn't work him much that fall.

Winnie still deployed on two more searches before officially retiring in the early spring of 2013. The next story is of one of those searches.

# Hellgate

Let me warn you right now, this isn't one of those happy ending searches. It was a suicide. Conrad Jordon left a note for his wife saying he was going to head down to the river to the Hellgate Overlook. He did just that and then parked his car overlooking the river canyon and jumped. It was Thursday December 6, 2012 and

*The Rogue River looking west from the Hellgate Overlook*

the monthly SAR members meeting was just concluding when Deputy Cory Krauss, our new SAR Coordinator, took a phone call and then briefed us all on the search slated for tomorrow morning. Mr. Jordan's car had been located exactly where he said he was going but he was nowhere in sight.

As we exited the meeting, I pulled Cory aside, "Hey Winnie is technically not certified but would you like me to bring him? and see what we can do?" "Oh sure, definitely." The response was quick with no hesitation.

I arrived a little early to avoid the contamination that would happen as soon as the rest of the searchers arrived. Being an overlook, the only place to park and set up command was at the last-known-point. It was a damp grey day, with temperatures in the high 30's. It had been raining heavily all along the west coast in early December, consequently the river was running high, just under flood stage, and it was the colour of brown frothing mud.

I got Winston ready and was provided a scent article that had been collected for me by the Sheriff as the vehicle had been towed the night before. The scent article was a pair of the subject's underpants. It became kind of a funny inside joke within the K9 Unit, because whenever the Sheriff collected a scent article for me it always seemed to be a pair of underpants. There was a photograph that was going around on the internet at the time of a bloodhound turning its nose up at some underwear and I've wondered if that is what provided the Sheriff's inspiration. Winston and I got started a bit after 0830 in the morning. Since we weren't out in the woods but instead along a well-travelled road, I worked alone.

I scented Winston while he was still in the vehicle, like I almost always do, and then walked him all around the parking area so he could take a quick inventory of the personnel on scene. I then more formally gave him scent – and his customary cookie – where the vehicle had been parked prior to it being towed. Rather than locate what we call an exit trail, Winston almost immediately went over to the decorative rock retaining wall in front of where the vehicle has been parked, put his front feet on and sniffed both the wall and the air intently. He performed the same behaviour on the same retaining wall immediately in front of a tourist placard, then again on the roadway's guardrail approximately 150 feet east of the parking area he sniffed deeply while leaning over the railing as best he could. I had a firm grip on the back of his harness. As I walked him both east and west from the parking lot, all he wanted to do was "go over" to the river's edge.

We only worked for 45 minutes but from Winston told me, our subject was below. I suggested that "teams thoroughly search either side of the overlook and along the riverbank just to the west of the overlook area."

As Winston and I were working the other searchers, including three air scent teams, arrived and were deployed. Then some weird stuff happened. The radio traffic between two of the air scent teams was fractured, tense, and quite honestly embarrassing. The tensions that started in the summer were boiling over and, while one of the teams stayed professional, the entire dialogue was not pretty to hear. And everyone could hear. Instead of pulling teams aside when they returned to base, I ignored it. In hindsight a big mistake on my part, as a little "behind the woodshed chat" was needed in that moment.

Our mountain rescue team started descending down into the canyon to search as best they could the crevice filled canyon wall. I put Winston up and suited up Beryl to take her down toward the river just west of the overlook. By walking west along the main road, we found a dirt track that afforded us easy access down to the swollen and muddy river. Lynda had arrived and flanked for me. For safety I was working Beryl in harness and on a long line. The river was not safe for man or beast and certainly not for "little B."

As we approached the river from the sandy and rocky trail that led from the track, Beryl started to exhibit body language indicators of being in odor. There was a small channel that had cut its way into the riverbank and was separated from the main river by stands of willow, now mostly flooded, and it was here that Beryl tried to enter the river. She was pulling so hard and fighting to get to the odor; she entered the channel as I held on and she tried to reach the stand of willows. She finally returned to shore and gave her trained indication. She pawed the ground and went into a down. Lynda flagged the area. We continued to work east (upriver) and she remained animated until we reached a sandy shore just below the overlook area. We then worked back west (downriver) and her body language again changed consistent with being in odor until we reached the end of the channel being formed by the brush where her body language changed again to "out of odor," and she desired to return upriver.

We were out only an hour. I recommended that our other HRD canine be brought in to search the area without letting on what Beryl had done. Her dog also alerted along the riverbank below the overlook.

Lynda and I led Deputy Kraus and Sergeant Richards (from Jackson County) back down toward the river where Beryl and Mara had alerted. Dawning personal flotation devices, the two officers entered the channel trying to reach the thick stand of willows to give them a more thorough search. A marine deputy stood by in his boat trying to hold his boat steady against the raging current. The river was ice-cold and dangerous and nobody was located trapped in the willows. For us, the search ended that day. Crews searched for two more day without success.

About a week later, someone in a boat spotted a body in a crevice along the rock wall. He was found just below Winston's furthest most point east. The negative.

It was a sad way to end the year. And sadly, our K9 Unit never again achieved that tight bond we once shared. We trained, we deployed in a professional manner but that sense of camaraderie, that closeness seemed to all but evaporated. The Unit actually started to split into little cliques. I seemed powerless to do anything about it. For the next 4.5 years or so that uneasiness remained and permeated into other aspects of search and rescue that I really enjoyed. One of those activities was teaching land navigation and search tactics to our new volunteers but also to hone the skills for everyone. In the end, that sour energy, was one of the reasons I decided to leave search and rescue all together. Not the only one, but the decision was made easier for me because of it.

----------

Winston was a funny dog in so many ways. He also was a bit of a Yoda. He taught me many things. One of the big topics of discussion among dog handlers, especially trailing dog handlers, has to do with the age of trails. How old is too old of a trail? On one extreme, some believe

that trailing dogs shouldn't even be deployed on trails over 6 hours old and on the other extreme are wild tales of weeks or months old trails. As usual, the truth often lies somewhere in between. I never hesitated deploying my dogs on "old" trails; many of our callouts occurred many hours or even days after the person went missing. The oldest I deployed on was six days but I would say most were a day or maybe two days old. Would or could Winston and later Tollie find such old trails? Maybe, maybe not, but that is often not the correct question in our wilderness setting. Could they detect the scent

of an individual person that had been missing in the wilderness for a day or for a few days. Yes. They proved over and over they could do that. Searching – regardless of the discipline the dog is primarily trained in, air scent or trailing – is all about hunting. If the dog relishes the hunt and wants to catch their prey (the lost person in this case) they will do so by any means.

If we listen to what our dogs are communicating, those invisible scent clues found along the way, and couple that with lost person behaviour and other data we now have powerful information to aid us in our search efforts. What do I mean? As SAR searchers we learn about lost person behaviour, where different types of people are commonly found, what they do when lost, that sort of thing. This is then paired with investigative clues, the terrain and climate, and all this information influences the direction of the search. It also influences what we do as searchers and canine handlers and how we devise the search strategy with our canine. We ask the question "What or Who are We Looking For?" Everything revolves around how we answer that question. We influence knowingly or unknowingly our canine partner. And they also show bias that influences what they do while searching. They are using learned associations to help them hunt their prey too. If in training, your training subject is always found in a drainage well then drainages become important to the dog. Same for placing HRD source in tree stumps; we now have given value to those locations. Dogs are using this locational information as well as olfaction to solve the puzzles in front of them. Both members of the canine team are thus searching and being influenced, to some degree, based on where they have had success before.

SAR K9 Winston

ShootingStar Raptor, NJP, CGC, SAR-W, PD, AKC ACE Nominee

(April 22, 2002 – Jan 4, 2017)

# TOLLIE

"And Deering's Woods are fresh and fair,
And with joy that is almost pain
My heart goes back to wander there,
And among the dreams of the days that were,
I find my lost youth again.
And the strange and beautiful song,
The groves are repeating it still:
'A boys will is the wind's will,
And the thoughts of youth are long, long thoughts.'"
Henry Wadsworth Longfellow

There were only a handful of searches in 2013; one of those lulls before the storm. My new puppy, Tollie, in the early months of 2013, passed his benchmark mantrailing evaluation at the tender age of nine-months. I was excited to be training a new puppy. My first puppy to train specifically for search and rescue since Beryl all those years ago. And she was two when she started!

By the time 2014 rolled around, Tollie was ready to certify for his mission ready status. I contacted the K9 Unit over in Jackson County and queried about a testing opportunity. I lucked out and a date was set. Test day dawned frosty cold but would give way to bright warm winter sunshine by the time the trail was ready for us, five hours later. I confidently casted Tollie around a huge old oak tree, the point-last-seen; it didn't take him long before he trotted off following the trail layer's scent. The line in my hand felt good, Tollie was doing great. Along a dirt track, I noticed head flicks indicating the direction we needed to go, a turn we needed to take, to reach our subject now hiding in the brush. Tollie found the turn and we headed across a huge pasture and then we reached a small hill with swirling winds, tricky scent dynamics that threw him off the trail. We eventually ended up on another hill above our quarry near the end of our time limit. I knew we were close. Do I cast him uphill or downhill? I had a 50/50 chance of getting it right. He took my lead and chased odor up the hill away from our hider. I was still very pleased, for a young dog he had performed admirably.

The evaluator that day made a notation in her report to me that read: *"Sorry the test didn't go as you had hoped but I am sure you and Tollie will retest soon and be successful. He is an amazing little working machine."* I tended to agree, he was quite an amazing little brown dog.

I was given another opportunity to test in April but it was just a few days after coming back from the Oso landslide with Beryl. Was I mentally prepared? I wasn't sure but I didn't want to have to reschedule. This time we got caught on a hill in the whirl of a scent pool created when our subject's scent rose like a chimney in the sun and then dropped and collected on the oak shaded hillside. Try as we might, we just could not break out of it. In discussing the track afterward, the evaluator apologized as he didn't think the test was set up very well with the way the hider had been reinserted into the end of the trail. I was beginning to get a little test phobic at this point. After the evaluation, Lynda who had come along to flank and support us, suggested we stop by one of our local wineries and have a glass of chardonnay. We just sat and talked about Oso, Tollie's test, the Unit and the conversation flowed from there. She knew I needed a shoulder more than I realized I did; I'm pretty good at shoveling things under the emotional rug until I am just exhausted. Such a simple gesture, "let's grab a glass of wine," she had said, turned into one of those memorable afternoons shared between friends.

*Lynda about to share her sandwich with K9 Tollie while taking a rest break while searching for Joyce Huffman*

# "That Was Easy"

Even before Tollie was officially certified he was allowed to participate in searches if they took place within Josephine County. According to Oregon Law (OS 404.110) "The Sheriff of each county has the responsibility for Search and Rescue activities within the county." In other words, the Sheriff can essentially choose to deploy or not deploy a team regardless of official certification status. Sheriff Gil Gilbertson trusted me and my silly funny quirky brown dogs and I always admired him as our County Sheriff. I was glad he had a good sense of humour too. So, when an elderly man disappeared while camping with his family over the long 2014 Fourth-of-July weekend far down a dusty and bumpy road (the 4612-098 road) near Sucker Creek, Tollie was welcome to participate.

----------

I had never been to the Sucker Creek drainage before and then twice that year I would find myself on searches in this rugged area. This search with Tollie would be my first introduction and then I would be back again in the fall as a ground searcher. During that second search, I was part of a three-person team responsible for hiking up the steep trail, measured at 23% in some places, to where the Sucker Creek trail intersected the Boundary trail to locate a young man and his dog; they had the foresight to stay put when they became confused on which way to go as the sun set on their day hike. As we descended the trail that dark night, it felt like something was following us. I turned around and one of our searchers had felt the same thing and had his sidearm out just in case. Both searches took place at night so I missed seeing some of the beauty of this rugged creek drainage.

That summer evening when the first call came, it was so hot down in the valley that I was looking forward to heading up into the mountains where maybe the air would be fresh and cool. As it was it was still probably in the mid 80's at near 9 pm when we commenced our search. We weren't the primary trailing team that night, that lead went to my friend Lynda and her dog, K9 Beezley. I had the privilege of coaching them as they got started in search and rescue and then observing their evaluation test held over at the coast. The test trail was a challenging one and they never missed a beat. I actually got goosebumps following along and watching this team pass their mission-ready test in May of the previous year. It was pure poetry in motion.

After collecting a scent article that night (a shoe belonging to Mr. Wallace) my flanker, Lucky, Tollie and I plus Lynda, K9 Beezley and Dave, her flanker, started our walk up the road toward the place Roy was last seen. Even though we walked as a group, both Lynda and I were still observing our dogs. Both Tollie and K9 Beezley were head checking toward the creek, something was tickling their senses. It was time to stop and scent my canine.

Since the PLS was just a spot along the dirt road and indistinguishable from the rest of the dirt road, our Sheriff had placed out a round light beacon that shone red in order to help searchers locate the exact spot. Tollie, who had just learned the trick of pushing the big red "That Was Easy" button promptly went over and stood on the light beacon. The light went out. Oops.

Lynda scented her canine and they began their search. I noticed they continued up the road. I waited about ten minutes before giving Tollie a chance to sniff the scent article again. We then commenced our search. From my official search report, I noted that:

Tollie exhibited behaviour consistent with trailing along the road from the dredge mining trail to the lower Sucker Creek TH. Several times he attempted to leave the road and proceed down toward the creek through the brush (my

196

flanker recorded these locations on his GPS); Tollie also did numerous head-checks toward the creek which is consistent with picking up scent. We checked the intersection of the spur road (which goes to the upper portion of Yew Creek) and Tollie gave a clear negative (no scent) on this spur road, FSR 540. When we reached the lower Sucker Creek trailhead (TH) we were asked to standby with lights off while a helicopter performed a search of the area. We waited in the dark for approximately 50 minutes.

Our Sheriff had marked the lower trailhead with another red beacon. Tollie went and stood on that one as well and oops, it too went dark. I was hopeful that our Sheriff had a good sense of humour.

Once we were given permission to continue our search, Tollie immediately took the trail down toward the creek and he was intent on following the Sucker Creek trail. I hesitated though, I knew that two air scent teams were in the area and confirmed with base that they had taken this trail to reach their search assignment. I now wasn't sure if Tollie was following them and knew that if they were ahead of me, surely, they would locate Mr. Wallace if he was along the trail. I, therefore, decided to caste him further up the 4612-098 road. We proceeded along the road for a short distance but I didn't observe any good trailing behaviour so we returned-to-base. It was now 0130 hours.

Based on the head checks, Tollie's interest in the Sucker Creek trail, thick vegetation and darkness limiting visibility along the creek itself, I suggested during the debrief that the creek drainage needed to be a priority once dawn broke.

It was the middle of the night now and we were so far down the narrow, rocky forest service road that a few of us chose to spend the night at base and get an early jump start on the next day's search efforts. I hunkered down in the back of Lynda's truck while Tollie slept soundly in his crate in my car. Tollie didn't deploy the next morning but instead I flanked for Lynda while she worked Beezley along the upper road after a possible footprint was discovered by a ground team. Fresh ground and canine teams arrived from the neighboring county and as we were preparing to leave for the day, the Jackson County SAR Coordinator asked me what I thought. "Along Sucker Creek below the road and between the lower and the upper trailheads was where I would place my bets," was my response. He thanked me and as we started walking down the road to our parked vehicles, we heard over the radio that Roy was okay. He emerged out of the drainage. He had spent the night in the drainage near the upper trailhead at the end of the road and had fallen asleep oblivious to the search going on all around him. A happy ending and I never heard from the Sheriff about the broken lights.

----------

A couple of months later, in the summer of 2014, we got a call about an overdue hiker in the Greyback Mountain area. There is no actual trail to Greyback Mountain, the trail only goes as far as the Boundary Springs trail where you can go left toward Sucker Creek or right and after many rough miles will lead to the town of Williams. Our subject's vehicle was parked at the O'Brien Creek upper trailhead that was reached by following a rutty gravel road that branched off to the west from Thompson Creek road (FSR 10). Tollie and I would work in tandem with Lynda and K9 Beezley. If our dogs split up at any decision point, then we would request ground support for each team. But for now, with so few resources, we didn't want to pull anyone off the one ground team's assignment. They were tasked with searching the upper meadow and the scree slope, the most logical route to take if you were planning on summiting Greyback Mountain. Greyback is the highest mountain in Josephine County with an elevation of just over 7,000 feet.

It's a two mile climb up to where the O'Brien Creek trail intersects the Boundary Springs trail and both dogs worked confidently as we climbed higher and higher along the steep switchback trail. At the turn off to the old Krause cabin, both dogs gave a firm negative indication that our missing person had not gone in that direction. As we intersected the Boundary Springs trail, the dogs did some circling in a small sunny, grass and flower filled meadow before exploring a thicket of trees to the south. After a short excursion into the trees, they turned themselves back around and we headed north instead toward Sugarloaf Peak. We took a rest on

*Taking a break just before intersecting the Boundary trail*

Sugarloaf and noted a footprint heading down a small path toward the town of Williams. This trail was not on our GPS or on our maps. As we began our descent, the radio crackled alive and our subject was okay and was safe. She had hiked herself out and was in Williams. Both Tollie and K9 Beezley had been on her trail! I was so proud of my young dog. He had stayed focused, on task, and had trailed our subject for over three miles up a mountain. He and Beez had worked together like this in training and it proved to work just as well on an actual deployment.

Tollie was deployed eight times before receiving his official certification papers. This next story is about that 8th deployment.

# One Special Night

For anyone who trains and works with animals there comes a time, either through a shared experience or maybe just a touching moment, when the relationship soars and an everlasting bond is formed. For Tollie and I, it was a search in the last weekend of November 2014, that provided just the right mix of ingredients to cement our relationship into something truly special.

All searches start pretty much the same; it is late at night and its pouring rain. This search would be no different; it was 1 am and a storm had made its way onshore. Tonight's search would start at the last-known-point (LKP) which happened to be the subject's vehicle. Mr. Bishop's pickup truck sat idle along the side of a potholed gravel Bureau of Land Management road on a switchback corner where, according to his wife, he would often park before going mushroom gathering in the thick damp woods. He and his friend shared this favorite spot, he usually worked on the right side of an unnamed creek drainage, his friend, now deceased, the left. Out of respect for his friend, he still gathered mushrooms only on the right side of the drainage. He liked to hike up toward the main ridgeline, which was a climb of roughly 1,300 feet. He was 65 years old and like so many, had some medical issues. His wife explained all of this as she sat in our operations/planning trailer, her eyes moist, her voice filled with concern. As I stood listening, the Sheriff turned to me and explained that the vehicle was locked but it had been cordoned off; so, with reassurance in his voice he looked back at the wife and told her he was sure my dog could still get a good whiff.

Dave, another canine handler, was my flanker, my support for the night. He noticed the back window of the Ford pickup was ajar. He was able to jimmy it open, reach in and unlock the driver's side door. Excellent. I was now able to collect a proper scent article. I chose to do a scent transfer as there was nothing actually in the cab of the pickup truck to use as a scent article – the only item being a towel that reportedly was used to dry his blue heeler cattle dog. To do this "scent transfer," I used a piece of 2 x 2 gauze and stuffed it into the crack between the seat and the backrest and, then after a minute or two, removed and placed the gauze piece into a plastic Ziploc baggie.

I scented Tollie while he was still in my vehicle. Base was going up all around us and I wanted "T" focused the minute he popped out of his car crate. He immediately took me to the pickup. I opened the driver's side door and he tried to climb in. I think he has it! He then worked around to the passenger side door and under the car. I went to caste him toward the small game trail beyond the blackberry vines and into the unnamed drainage but he stood firm "strong scent right here!" Silly dog I thought as Dave instinctively searched for a hidden set of car keys. Tollie then acquiesced to my suggestion of where to start our search and into the dark damp forest we went. He worked along the swollen creek for about 500 feet and then he started head checking to the right. He finally stopped, came back past me, crossed the creek and launched himself up the opposite bank. And UP we went!

We worked up the steep slope, zigzagging at times across a ridgeline. We crossed old skid roads, now mostly overgrown but still discernable even in the limited light of our headlamps. Dave then noticed a mushroom stem lying on the ground that had most likely been cut. Base confirmed that our missing subject had a butter knife with him. A clue? Possibly. Several times Tollie would suddenly start circling an area, checking odor at the base of trees, in the leaf litter, on the ground adjacent to downfall, all places where wild mushrooms like to grow. He would work these small scent pools for several minutes before locating an exit trail and continuing upward. Tollie was also "playing" the steep draw on the left (northwest) side as we climbed higher in the dark.

It was physically challenging but I didn't notice. Tollie was at the end of my 40-foot line but we were connected by more than a piece of biothane; at night, you just have the feel of the line, the feel of your surroundings, and when you let go and stop being afraid of the dark, of the dangers, of falling and failing, and trust in your partner and yourself, the night, the rain, the woods all become just part of who you are at the moment. It's a strange kind of freedom. As we neared the top of the ridge, Tollie's pace quickened, and his behaviour told us he had a nose full of scent or what we call a proximity alert. Dave then noticed a CD case hanging from a branch in a tree. A marker of some kind? Then, in a flash we were in a clearing high on the ridge top and we heard yelling. Was it the ground team working down from the top ridgeline? Was it our Mr. Bishop? It was both.

"I'M DOWN HERE!"

Over the radio, the ground team asks: "K9, can you reach the subject? You appear closer."

We reply, "we are attempting to find a safe route down but appear to have a cliff to work around," and we encouraged the ground team to proceed.

A few minutes pass as we try to navigate the slick rocky slope and then we hear the ground team over the radio: "Subject has been located and is doing fine!"

Dave and I look at each other and its high fives all around. Hugs to the "T-man."

It's been three hours since we started our search. Three exacting hours. Three exceptional hours. And our journey was not yet complete for we had to get down back down the over 1,000 feet we had just climbed, in the dark, in the relentless pouring rain, and soon without any working GPS.

Once we heard the radio communication from the ground team that they had successfully negotiated the steep slope and made contact with the lost, but now found, subject we started to head back toward base. We decided backtracking was going to be most prudent rather than attempt to meet up and walk out with the ground team plus they needed to get the subject safely back to base and not wait for us to get down the slope. We checked coordinates, took a bearing, radioed in our intentions and off we went. Simple.

*The area we searched in that night and where my GPS was lost and then found*

About 100 feet into our descent, however, I noticed that my chest pack was missing a GPS unit. I tried to retrace my steps but finding a black and orange GPS among the leaf litter of autumn and dark tree trunks and downfall was not going to happen. Dave marked the area on his unit and we joked about coming back in a day or two to retrieve my GPS.

At this time Dave noticed that his unit was low on battery power and by an unlucky coincidence we didn't have any spare batteries. Dave's GPS then went dark as the night. Not a problem, how hard could it be to walk downhill retracing an earlier path.

We were doing just fine and actually crossed old skid roads and other land marks that we noticed on the way up. It then got really steep (we couldn't have come up this?) and so we veered southeast to where the slope appeared gentler which pulled us around and over a ridge and into a neighboring drainage. We walked into a small meadow, something we hadn't encountered on the trek up. We radioed base and sort of jokingly asked them to sound a car horn to see how close we were and to get our bearings. Only we didn't hear a thing.

The drainage we now found ourselves in was steep and narrow and we had to backtrack several times to inch our way downward. Instead of pulling ahead of me on his trailing line, Tollie kept pace with me somehow realizing that for humans it's apparently much more difficult to travel down a steep slope than it is to travel up. "What was that?" I asked Dave. "It sounded like a growl," he replied. Tollie growled back into the dark. Whatever it was, it stayed hidden in the brush and we continued down through the slippery mud. Ted, a member of the SAR Vehicle Unit, started driving the road sounding the jeep horn to help guide us down the mountain. Back and forth he went until we radioed "yes, that is the loudest blast yet!" "I have your drainage pinpointed and will wait for you on the road," he radioed back.

We carefully entered the narrow creek bed choked full of downfall, rocks, and huge trees. Tollie carefully negotiated his way and never strayed too far ahead of me as if he knew the going was tough and the hour was late. Soon enough we were back on the road, a nice warm ride waiting to take us back to base. It was now 0600.

It was just one night, not a particularly hard night really, we had been out for only five hours but in the odd ways of human-canine communication, Tollie and I became closer, we matured on the trail as a solid working team, our trust was solidified, our love cemented. As we rode back to base, he snuggled next to me on the rear seat of the

SAR jeep, leaning into me with his shoulder, teammates. We done good little man.

Four days later, the lost GPS was successfully recovered.

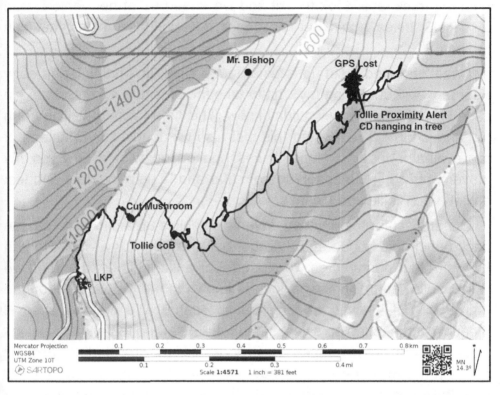

I had another opportunity to test in late January of 2015. This was a double-blind evaluation to be held up in the Myers Camp area. Although I requested my last two evaluations be double-blind, they turned out to be single-blind, not that it made any difference in the outcome. A double-blind test best mimics a real search as no one, not even the evaluator, knows where the test subject is hiding and how they got there. This third evaluation test was yet another fail. I made a mistake and pushed my dog into a scent pool that he successfully extricated himself from and he was back on the trail looking very solid and confident. Right near the very end, however, he missed the acute angle turn of "the fresher" reinsertion track, and instead he continued on the path my track layer took to exit and we ended up at her vehicle. Bad test luck strikes again but those are real-world situations that can happen.

I was frustrated. I set up a test about a week and half later, in early February, without telling my Unit to take the pressure off myself and in case I failed again they wouldn't know. This time I was travelling north to Lane County. I requested this test also be double-blind. Instead of my evaluator tagging along, I was hooked up with a GPS so my movements could be observed from afar and to help me deal with test anxiety. So, Tollie and I went solo.

Our subject for the day had driven his vehicle up a dirt track that ran back behind his house and then got out and went for a walk. He had been out four hours when we started. Tollie lifted his head and off we went. I followed trailing behaviour, unknown to me we were not on the trail at all but he was working just the same. We crossed a small meadow and headed up a very steep track. I saw no footprints, no signs of any recent activity. Then Tollie took me into the darkest thickest drainage I ever been in. The trees and brush hid the sunlight; there wasn't a lot of ground cover just sticks of leafless trees. It felt like I was trapped and being smothered in a bamboo forest, everything closing in around me. As I struggled with the line, my mental strength, my belief in myself started to fade and I sat down and cried. I could not fail again. I had to believe in my ability and I knew I could trust my partner. I asked myself if this were a search, what would I do? I looked at my map. I had noted areas where we had strong scent, I just needed to get out of this trap we had been sucked into. I got on the radio and let my evaluator know that I was exiting the drainage and heading back to a place where Tollie had lifted his head as scent probably had dribbled down the mountain. "Fine, sounds good' was the cheerful response. Caroline is always cheerful.

I took Tollie back to the place where he had strong scent, I had marked this spot on my GPS like I had done so many times during actual deployments, and he headed uphill. It was a bloody steep hill. The ferns and holly were so thick that I could barely see Tollie as he bulldozed through and found another dirt track. He turned a corner and ran further up the hill and there sitting next to a tree was our lost subject.

# Difficult Conversations

2015 and 2016, like 2014, were busy years. One of K9 Tollie's first searches after being certified was a search in Jackson County for an elderly man who had been out collecting pinecones.

Sunday March 16th, 2015. David Froling, 83 years old, drove his trusty Ford F-150 up to the Willow Prairie Horse Camp area and parked at the end of the 200 road, a dirt road that just ended after roughly one-half mile. He grabbed his white bucket, his dog, locked his keys in the car, and went in search of knobcone pinecones which he used for crafting. When he didn't return home that evening, his family alerted search and rescue. CORSAR teams were called in to assist late Monday afternoon.

It was a mild day with temperatures in the mid-40's when we arrived at near five o'clock in the afternoon and checked in at the Incident Command Post (ICP), set up at the Willow Lake Horse Camp. Wind was light from the southwest as Dave, my flanker, and I drove to the end of the 200 road in order to start our assignment. During the day a white bucket had been found just south of where Mr. Froling's vehicle was parked, and I was asked to start my trailing dog from the bucket and attempt to get a direction of travel. I first needed to collect a scent article. Although the keys were locked in the truck cab, Dave discovered the back shell cover was unlocked and I was able to collect a wool cap that I could use to scent my dog.

Dave and I had the bucket location entered into our GPS units so we navigated easily to where it had been found. I stopped about 25 feet from the bucket and formally presented Tollie the scent article. Tollie immediately went over to investigate the bucket. Tollie took us west a short distance before circling back to the subject's vehicle where he alerted on the vehicle by placing his paws up on the vehicle and sniffing intently. At least I knew that I had a good scent article. Tollie then took us east along the dirt road but again he circled back to the vehicle. Finding an "exit trail" was proving difficult.

K9 Tollie finally entered the woods and worked initially south and then toward the east in a back-and-forth manner as if working a large widespread scent cone rather than exhibiting trailing behaviour. At UTM 10T 0549664E 4695821N 6:52:05 PM, K9 Tollie lifted his head and scented the wind which was coming from a southerly direction, and exhibited classic long-distance alert behaviour.

I had seen this behaviour so many times before. Tollie was literally dancing on the tip of his paws trying to reach the scent blowing towards him and out of his reach. He was even trying to climb the trees. We circled manically around this area but came up empty. Dave and I both shot a bearing on the wind direction and like we both so often did also took a mental note of the wind direction as we made a mental map of our surroundings. We continued a bit further to the east but Tollie then changed direction back to the west and also started to bend directly south and into the wind. As we began descending into Willow Prairie through trees so dense that making headway became difficult, his behaviour changed again but this time he was out of scent; just then we also met a large ground team heading north from the exact direction we were headed. I mentioned to one of the ground team members that we had been working scent and we were being pulled south; the response was a flippant "your dog was probably just scenting us." I felt deflated, this wasn't the first time that peers had caste negative comments in our direction and clearly it was affecting my attitude. After this encounter, we concluded our search efforts. It was only 8 pm. We turned around and headed back to where I had parked my car, a short distance from the Mr. Froling's pickup truck.

Just as we were about to depart and head back to ICP we heard the distinct sound of a dog barking in the distance. The direction of the sound was coming from the southeast. About three minutes later a helicopter arrived on scene and we could no longer hear the dog. We agreed that the dog bark sounded like alarm barking.

All of our information was relayed to Command during the formal debrief process. I suggested the area southeast of the bucket in the direction of both the barking and the air scent "alert" behaviour be thoroughly searched. I was then asked to draw a circle of "where to search" on the master planning map. I drew a circle about ½ mile from where Tollie showed his strong change of behaviour. The gentleman debriefing me rolled his eyes. In hindsight, I hadn't quite drawn the line far enough.

Mr. Froling was discovered deceased by a K9 air scent team the following day on the same heading but just a tad further "out" than the circle I had drawn the evening before. The other interesting bit was that he was located at roughly the same elevation as when Tollie showed his unmistakable change of behaviour. Scent had most likely been carried across and above the prairie which was at a slightly lower elevation.

As canine handlers and as a K9 Unit we frequently performed formal and informal post search analysis. Could we have done better? Did we make any mistakes? Every search dog handler goes through this process and sometimes you don't like what you uncover. I've made mistakes. There have been times, like this search, that I question my decisions. Why did we stop? Could we have gone further? Could I have better conveyed to command what my dog was so clearly communicating to me? As Unit Leader I noticed that one of our air scent canines had been exceptionally close to Mr. Froling that Monday evening. According to GPS readings, very, very close. Was it a miss by the dog or by the handler not reading their dog (missing their dogs

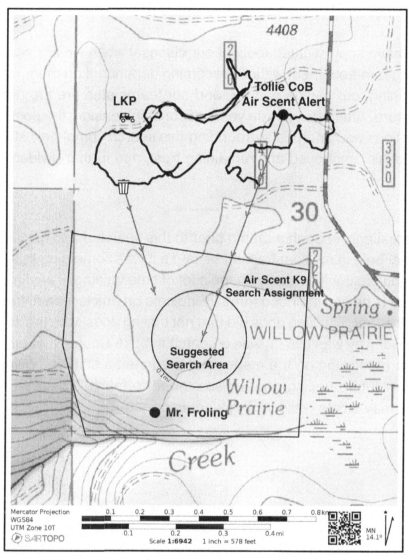

tells)? Perhaps the wind conspired against the team. Was there a training hole or was it just really bad luck? Would the outcome had been any different? Many questions with no definitive answers and all done without fault or blame. That said, it's a hard conversation to have. I've had these conversations with myself many, many times – they play over and over in my head. It's hard to let those ghosts go, if you ever really can.

We have sophisticated tools at our disposal when we are searching, we can learn from them without becoming dependent on them. Trusting our training, our canine partner, and our teammates are the real tools to treasure. After nearly three years of constant tension, the post search discussions and analysis surrounding this search completely shattered a friendship, destroyed any remaining trust, and further divided the K9 Unit.

----------

Interestingly enough a month prior to this search, I had discovered a potential hole in my own training because it was something that trailing dog handlers don't normally spend a lot of time training, if anytime at all. And that is having their dog formally indicate on articles, potential clues, along the trail. Tracking dogs did that not trailing dogs, was the accepted norm. But why was this? It was a search in Lake County that began my change of thinking on the matter and prompted a shift on how I would start any future trailing dog. I also started to teach Tollie that articles that he may locate while trailing were important.

# Quartz Pass

Like so many of our searches, the circumstances of how and why a person has gone missing is never straightforward. I received an email from the Lake County K9 Unit Lead the evening before we were to set travel the roughly 175 miles to search for a 44-year-old male named Spencer. She shared with me with some extra details of what had been discovered on the first day of the search which might not be included in the general briefing. When I first started in SAR, the county K9 Units didn't really have relationships where they would talk and share information but after the Kim Search, the formation of CORSAR and, honestly, some personality changes over time, that changed for the better. The various county K9 Units now trained together and when there was a CORSAR search, information was shared on what the dogs did and any clues that were discovered so new arriving teams had just a little bit more information that what was usually shared in the pre-search briefing. I had all evening and a few hours in the morning during the drive to try and make sense of what had been shared.

Spencer was reported to be in good physical condition with excellent outdoor experience and would often go for long jaunts where he doesn't contact family. He had, for example, walked through the wilds of Asia for several months. He did have mental struggles, however, but was not thought to be dangerous to himself or to others. On Friday the 13th, he tried to turn his motorhome around on the 3660 road about ½ mile north of Quartz Mountain Pass and Highway 140. He got stuck. It was 1130 in the morning when some kind folks stopped by to help; he was doing fine but they let him know that they were going to go home and return with a larger truck to help pull him out. When they returned, the motorhome was still there but he wasn't around anywhere. They checked back again before dark and he still wasn't at his motorhome.

Spencer had two dogs with him, both cherished yellow Labrador retrievers. Bella was nine years old while Angel was only four. On Saturday, another couple travelling through the area noticed a yellow lab beside the side of the road and when they retraced their steps a couple hours later the dog was still there and started following their car. They picked up Bella. There was no sign of Angel. They were roughly 1.5 miles north of the motorhome which was now burned. Sometime between Friday and Saturday it had caught fire and was completely destroyed. How it caught fire no one knew. Investigators did confirm that there were neither human or canine remains in the burned motorhome.

Searchers spent all day Sunday searching for Spencer and his Labrador. Boot and dog tracks and even dog feces were found along the road but did they belong to him and Angel? A cliff bar wrapper was discovered, did it belong to Spencer? More boot tracks were found off the road heading further north by K9 Finn and his handler Gail but soon the track went cold. Other material clues, a balaclava and nail clippers, were found along the road about 200 meters north of the motorhome, which were presumed to be his. So many potential clues.

It was now Tuesday the 16th of February, four days since anyone had seen Spencer. Since the motorhome was destroyed, the family had been instructed to bring some items of his to be used by the canines as scent articles. The previous April, almost a year prior, the family boxed up some of his belongings and they brought those stored items to help with the search. I chose two scent articles from the box, a shoe and a shoe insole. The shoe, a croc-style shoe was reportedly his favorite, and the insole I chose came from a set of hiking boots. With Lynda as support that day we headed over to the point-last-seen (PLS). Because I knew so many potential clues were found along the road north of the

214

motorhome, I wanted to be extra cautious that I did not suggest a direction to my dog so after acclimatizing Tollie to the area by walking him around for a few minutes, I formally scented him about 50 feet south of the motorhome.

My search notes indicate he proceeded directly to the burned motorhome and then continued around a cattle guard. He proceeded only a short time along the main road before turning back toward the PLS and ultimately heading east over a small hill. Near the crest of the hill, he showed some head-up air scenting behaviour as he was working the wind.

Tollie ultimately led us over the small hill into the placid draw of Quartz Creek. Lynda and I commented to each other that it felt like we were working proximity scent, that maybe our subject was near, maybe watching us and definitely evading us. During out initial briefing we were informed that Spencer did have some mental health issues, specifically paranoid tendencies and could be schizophrenic. It was also suggested during our briefing that instead of calling for him that we call out the name of his dog. From my search report:

As we proceeded east down the hill, we noted at UTM 10 T 0681126E 4688051N, 5581 ft, 12:27:46 PM what appeared to be very fresh thrown up grass, like a dog might do (subject had two dogs with him - one subsequently was located). K9 Tollie continued into the Quartz Creek draw and with favorable wind, headed due north along and paralleling a very muddy dirt track. At UTM 10 T 0681447E 4688110N, 5491 ft, 1:10:48 PM, Tollie took notice of and sniffed intently at something on the ground. It was a receipt from a Safeway Grocery Store. The receipt date read Jan 16, 2015, exactly one month ago, and is in virtually pristine condition as if it had just fallen out of a pocket.

Following standard protocol, we called our potential clue into Command, and they instructed us to collect the receipt and bring it back to base with us when we completed our assignment.

215

Tollie continued working hard northward until we reached a place called Ewauna Camp. K9 Tollie then proceeded east along the main road, checking the steep hillside to the north of the 3660 road but not showing any desire to proceed up the hill. We noted previous searchers had marked a track in this area. It was also just north of here that on Saturday, Bella had been picked up by some good Samaritans along the road. By the time we reached the cattle pens, Tollie was tired. We had covered about 3.5 miles at this point and he seemed to have lost the trail along the road. I chose to return-to-base.

*K9 Tollie working hard along the trail*

Did the receipt we found belong to Spencer or had it just been dropped the previous day by searchers that may have been in the area? It was investigated but the answers were inconclusive. We would never find out, as Spencer was eventually located deceased about one month later. Angel was still with him, watching over his body.

----------

Clues. One of the things we teach our new searchers is that there are always more clues out there than the lost person. Mantrackers know this all too well. I know that I trained Beryl to tell me about potential clues she may come across while searching, things like backpacks, or items of clothing but none of my mantrailing dogs had ever been taught to indicate on such clues. What if I had? Would Winnie have alerted on the tree he sniffed so closely during the Twin Lakes search? Would Tollie had alerted on the grocery receipt? It was after this search that I began to teach Tollie about articles, that they were important, that if he sniffed them and they belonged to the missing, I wanted to know about them. When I started to teach my new puppy in 2018, I started her first on teaching her a strong article indication. This was also key to shaping her precision tracking skills.

Our dogs also provide other tangible clues and not just scent related but behavioural as well. When Tollie was a wee pup he fell into his breeder's duckweed covered garden pond. Tollie was not impressed and he was my first Sussex who really didn't care about water and to this day I have never seen him swim. Oh, he will wade in on hot day but his feet will always be touching the bottom. As a young dog it was actually Beezley that showed him how to cross a creek when we stopped to cool the dogs near La Pine, Oregon on our way to Summer-Ex at Diamond Lake. Suffice to say, if Tollie wanted to enter water, especially a rushing river, it meant something.

# Two Trails

I know I am not alone; I know others write to release those thoughts that replay like a bad dream in one's head over and over until sleep becomes impossible. I, therefore, apologize to you, my somewhat captive audience for this rambling tale but, on the off-chance you find this story a trifle bit interesting then I will have, as they say, "killed two birds with one stone." Where to start? Well, let's just say it had been a bad couple of days. Real bad. On one cold mid-February day alone, two friends passed away in addition to my husband's uncle; then I learned another friend suffered a stroke, and yet another was diagnosed with cancer. And then a man I never met walked away from his care home in the dead of the night, in the pouring rain, never to be seen again.

This story really begins, to be more precise, a few weeks before that rainy cold February weekend. It begins, in fact, a couple of days after Christmas 2015. It was then that a young man with Huntington's disease living in a rather nondescript care home tucked away in the woods disappeared sometime before the sun rose on a cold grey wintery morning, the falling snow gently coating the frozen ground. My phone rang just as dawn was breaking with the news and I climbed out of bed with the usual adrenalin rush breaking through the fog of a deep sleep. First things first, flip the coffee pot switch to on. In the ten or so minutes it took me to get dressed, load Tollie and Beryl in the car, and make sure my teammates were notified the coffee was brewed and I poured a large cup into my travel mug and headed north to our SAR building, a 30-minute drive away. I only stopped there long enough to recruit my support person and grab a map of the area. It was then back in my car and over the first mountain pass on I-5 north of town and into the small community of Sunny Valley. We spotted an Oregon State Police (OSP) vehicle idling by the side of the road near the town's historic covered bridge. I assumed the trooper, who was sitting warmly in his vehicle, was hoping the man would just wander by as he had a reputation for hitch hiking when he had gone missing on previous occasions. A little further along the road was our Bureau of Land Management (BLM) Deputy who stopped us so we could get an updated briefing prior to driving the last bit to the care home. It was starting to snow harder now and I was anxious to get started. I drove down the rutted gravel driveway and pulled up to the tidy house surrounded by thick woods where the owner came out to meet us. After asking a few questions we were escorted to the man's room so I could collect a good scent article. Today, I chose a worn sock that was lying on the floor. We were the only personnel on scene when I harnessed and scented Tollie; he jumped out of my car, into the cold, and went to work.

With nose down Tollie headed back down the driveway but after less than 100 yards he stopped and circled and found the corner he was searching for and we slipped through a narrow opening in a tall wooden fence after squeezing behind a truck parked purposefully to impede passage. Weaving through the woods we emerged into a marijuana grow, now dormant for the winter, and then started down an embankment to a neighboring property where we spied a small pond, a flooded pasture, a flock of turkeys, and smoke rising from an old farmstead. We stopped as my support went to receive permission to cross into the property, otherwise we did risk being shot. This is rural Oregon after all. Almost half mile later, we emerged on the road we had driven in on and Tollie turned assuredly north. And then his head rose high in the air, his whole body lifting upward trying to reach the scent being held and carried by the wind, the scent he was chasing, the scent of the missing. He dragged me across the bridge spanning swollen Graves Creek and circled back under the bridge. The creek was in full flood, brown angry water. It had rained nearly every day that month, the rainiest December on record. Even normally benign creeks were now dangerous and raging. Tollie isn't too keen on water but he pulled me across the slippery rocks to sniff the vegetation at the water's edge and then he tried to enter the creek, only the line holding him back. Tollie showed no trailing behavior beyond this point. Was our missing man in the creek? Had he been picked up by a passing vehicle? We didn't know. Would we ever know what happened? Had we done enough? It was just shy of three weeks later when the man's body was discovered some two miles downstream.

----------

Then at the end of January 2016, SAR personnel from several counties and hundreds of emergent volunteers, almost all from the small close-knit running community, spent three days searching for a long-distance runner who went missing doing what he did almost every day, running the mountain trails above Ashland. This search ended like so many recently, sadly. The young man was found deceased in the creek that runs through the heart of this beautiful southern Oregon town which bears the same name; the creeks headwaters on the highest peak in the Siskiyou Mountains, Mt. Ashland. So, when the call came that mid-February night that a man with Alzheimer's was missing the adrenaline was high, the sense of urgency overpowering for everyone responding; we just had to find this man and bring him home to his family. We all desperately needed a story with a happy ending.

The call came during that time of night when nothing stirs, after even the hardiest have gone to bed and well before even the earliest of the early risers start to stir. I arrived on scene at 0200 and again, I was the first SAR person on scene. I saw OSP, in their familiar and distinct vehicles, driving the roads searching, as I drove through the neighborhood before turning onto a familiar street (yes, we had been

220

here before for a search & rescue mission). Instead of snow this evening, however, it was raining and raining hard. Although no Law Enforcement was at the house, the conditions made it imperative that I not wait around before deploying. The man was elderly, suffered from Alzheimer's and was probably only dressed in a nightshirt. Having a good scent article is always critical for the scent discriminating trailing dog and finding one in a care home can be a challenge as clothing is usually washed together and things could get handled by just about anyone. In this case I spied a hat on the bookcase style headboard behind the subject's bed. "Does he wear that often?" I quired. "All the time," came back the reply. With gloved hands I placed the Korean War Veteran hat in a large Ziploc bag and carried it out to my vehicle. As I was stepping out the front door, a relative of the subject stopped me and asks "I hope I haven't messed things up, but I've been out looking for him and I am wearing his jacket." I mumbled something back trying to be reassuring. Tollie's job just got a bit more challenging.

Like I usually do, I scented Tollie while he is still in my vehicle so he is ready to immediately go to work as soon his paws hit the ground. He circled around the front lawn of the home and started working his way toward some bushes that marked the boundary of a neighboring property when one of the care home's four golden retrievers came charging across the lawn barking at us. Tollie glanced up and looked at the loud charging dog and then quietly went right back to work. Just one of the hazards of urban searches. Tollie found the man's scent trail and he followed it toward the neighbor's house and continued through a grassy side yard to the back garden and to a decorative retaining wall enclosing a small patio. When he got to the wall, his nose rose and he carefully smelled the top of the wall before jumping on top and looking down to the Rogue River below – rushing at over 7,000 cubic feet per second that night – and then the trail just stopped. I headed back to the care home and queried the jacket wearing relative to see where he had searched for his missing family member. What I discovered was that he had not gone over to the neighbor's property in question and instead had walked down the dead-end street in the opposite direction.

As I rested my dog briefly, other SAR personnel arrived on scene. I briefed our SAR Coordinator on our efforts but said that I wanted to go back out there. I was hoping Tollie had been wrong. I even went so far as to collect another scent article – this time one of the subject's shoes. I also now had a support person to assist me. I again started Tollie from the back of my vehicle and then casted him wide to ensure he had taken in all the scents even those across the street from the care facility. He did just that but turned around and headed back to the care home, this time going around to the back sliding door on the rear porch (the alarm on this door had been triggered four hours earlier by the now missing man) and then with nose down certainty he trailed along a small gravel path along the side of the house and into the neighbor's property, just like he had done earlier, and right back to the that same garden wall overlooking the swollen river. I had my flanker gingerly picked his way down the 20 feet of embankment to the river's edge to see if there were any footprints in the small patch of wet sand. An indentation perhaps but we were unsure. Tollie circled back to this very spot twice more, each time with more confidence that the trail just ended here. In daylight

the next day, Tollie jumped over the wall and tried to enter the river.

The search continued for three full days in the never-ending rain with no sign of the missing.

*K9 Beryl working from the bow of the boat during the search for the missing kayaker*

A week or so later a body was discovered in the river but was identified as that of a missing kayaker that we had searched for one month earlier. Beryl, working from the bow of our marine boat, had alerted on an eddy in the river during that search but the Rogue was running too high and fast to put divers in the water. In the month or so since he had been missing, the river had carried his body 13 miles from where he was last scene.

It wasn't until mid-March that the mighty Rogue River, still swollen by heavy rains, unleashed her grip on the elderly man. A body was spotted, caught in the brush just above the river's edge near a place called Foster Bar Camp, some 70 miles downstream from Grants Pass. That vegetation along the river's edge allowed a family to have their dad, their husband, their granddad back. From Foster Bar it's not really that much further to the Pacific Ocean.

As a searcher, having some kind of resolution is important, not knowing can be hard on us too. No longer having to wonder late at night if we missed something or could have done something different or better is somehow comforting.

*Tollie trying to keep his feet dry*

# A Much Happier Ending

I was standing on a ladder in my kitchen wearing slippers with a scrapper in one hand and a hot water filled water spray bottle in the other desperately trying to remove dated and ugly wallpaper when the pager blared its ringtone at me. "Sh*t" was my first thought; I had only one-quarter of the wall left to do and I was on a mission to remove every last scrap of the hideous paper. I'd also been working on it for well over 10 hours and I didn't want to stop for anything. Quick check of the message, "missing camper in the Secret Creek area, report to SAR." Wilderness search, my favorite type of callout. Duty calls, the wall would have to wait.

Secret Creek, about a 1 ½ hour drive from my house, is a beautiful little spot in the Rogue River Siskiyou National Forest and quit near a favorite training and camping spot of mine. I figured that the subject would probably self-rescue before we even arrived but if he hadn't then this could be a long day or days search. What often happens is after spending a miserable night in the woods, the lost person finds an old logging road and makes their way safely "out" which coincidently had just happened the previous day about three miles north of Secret Creek at a place called Horse Creek. We were holding canine training at Horse Creek and one of our handlers, coming up a bit later, located the subject walking along the road as he was driving up to alert us to the search. Of course, there is no cell service in this area.

After stopping at SAR briefly, I headed up the twisty one lane mountain road to meet up with our BLM Deputy who was overseeing the SAR mission that day. After a quick briefing, I was escorted to the campsite to collect a scent article. Our subject had been camping at this spot for about two weeks and he and his friends had been riding dirt bikes in the area and just sort of hanging out. "He may be a bit depressed, he's been missing for over 24 hours, and he has a shotgun with him which might have been fired during the night," his friend casually mentioned.

From the campsite, there was one gravel road which exited onto an open grassy area where four roads and a trail intersected. Which way did he go? I got started as soon as I could because SAR personnel, a command vehicle, ATVs, and other equipment were all just arriving and you can guess where everyone was parking!

Once harnessed and scented, Tollie got right down to work. He worked right through all the commotion of a SAR base going up around him and entered the woods near the trail head. His head was high as he picked up pockets of odor. I noticed the hillside here had been beat up with dirt bike tracks so I knew our subject had been here but when had he been here? After a short distance, Tollie headed through a thicket of wild hazelnut, fresh bear droppings underfoot, until we arrived back on the main road. Tollie turned back toward the command area and again worked right through the people and vehicles and took us down a small dirt track that headed toward to the creek. A car and a tent were adjacent to the creek but Tollie showed no interest in either (I learned afterward that a young woman was asleep in the tent even though it was now noon) and he entered the creek momentarily. After a quick sip of water, or was it a taste, we continued along the dirt track. And then wham, the head was up and he had a nose full of scent. In a flash, he leaped over a log and dropped 3 feet into the creek and swam to the other side. I knew he had our man but my heart sank briefly thinking about those recent searches that had ended so tragically at water's edge. As Tollie exited the creek on the opposite side of where we stood, he pushed through about 20 feet of skunk cabbage and then started to head up the steep hillside before turning back and recrossing

225

the creek and now pulling me through thick vine maple. And then I saw a little movement about 10 feet ahead of me and called out our subject's name and got a weak reply. I could barely see him and he was right in front of me. I put the brakes on Tollie and my support quickly took over. Oh my gosh, I had never trained for stopping Tollie and not allowing him to go into the subject. Sussex can PULL!!!! I couldn't allow him to go in for we had to assess medical condition and ascertain safety; the man was holding a loaded shotgun. We were only about 300 feet from his camp but the subject of our search had no idea where he was; he was dehydrated and confused and his feet were dangling in the cold creek waters.

I got on the radio, "subject located!" Good boy Tollie, good boy.

----------

### Search and Rescue Team Locates Missing Camper on Secret Creek on Saturday

Josephine County Search & Rescue crews located a missing camper on Saturday. The Josephine County Sheriff's Office received a report about a 49-year-old man who was missing from a camp at Secret Creek, which is located in the Siskiyou National Forest in the Briggs Valley area.

Deputy Jason Stanton said the missing person was camping with friends and was last seen at midnight on Thursday. The friends spent all day Friday looking for him and called the Sheriff's Office for help on Saturday morning. The friends believed they needed to wait 24 hours before reporting a missing person.

Deputy Stanton said Josephine County Search & Rescue immediately responded to Secret Creek and started searching for the missing person. He said Search & Rescue K-9 "Tollie" located the missing man along the creek at 12:45 p.m.

The unidentified man told officials he left camp at 9 a.m. Friday for a short hike, but did not tell anyone he left camp or where he was going. When he was located, he was not injured and declined medical attention before being returned to camp.

The Josephine County Sheriff's Office would like to remind everyone a 24-hour waiting period is not required before reporting a missing person or lost subjects. In addition, the Sheriff's Office would like to thank the hard work and dedication of the Search & Rescue team – which is primarily staffed by volunteers. Posted on 5/2/16 8:19AM by Sam Marsh

*Getting found by*
*Mr. Tollie*

# Yellow Submarine

It was a good spring for another team in our K9 Unit, K9 Beezley and her handler Lynda would have their first live find as well.

Per usual, the call came near midnight. As I arrived on seen, it was just myself and our SAR Deputy. A women identified as Lauren Page has wandered away from her home just off Redwood Highway. This highway, also known as 199, is a two-lane heavily traveled highway between southern Oregon and California and is also the safest way to access the southern Oregon coast. If only the Kim family had taken this road all those years ago now. Our Deputy conducted the standard interview and learned that Lauren had last been seen about twelve hours earlier by her husband. She had taken some newly prescribed medications that were perhaps not mixing well with some other prescribed medications. She was apparently a bit paranoid and unsettled. She often walked and visited her neighbor; her home was immediately to the east but they were away. I was asked to go ahead and get started with Tollie and just then Lynda arrived and offered to assist in flanking.

I began the search in the front yard before other searchers arrived and the area became contaminated. Tollie circled a bit and took me to some wooden steps leading to the back door. He spent some time here and then confidently headed down the driveway as search vehicles headed up the steep paved driveway. At the bottom of the driveway was a "T." Would we go left, east toward the neighbor's property, or bend right toward Redwood Highway. He circled a bit here just as an Oregon State Police vehicle exited the neighbor's fenced property. Seeing this as our opportunity to gain easy access, I helped Tollie make up his mind in which way to go and with a slight tug on the line suggested that we go through the open gate. I never like to suggest a direction but it had been stressed she liked to visit the neighbors, so I let that information influence what happened next. As we entered the property, the electric gate shut behind us. Lynda and I exchanged a look, "that might be a problem."

It was a fairly large property with a stream behind the house. Tollie was not finding a trail but he did catch some scent blowing from the direction of the Highway. He even tried to go through the fence on that south side of the property. We needed to head that direction but we were now behind an electronic gate! How to get out? The keypad was on the other side of the fence. We ended up pulling the pin on the gate and making a quick exit. I felt too much time had elapsed since Tollie's desire to get out of the property and our own extrication from the predicament we found ourselves in so suggested we switch dogs out and work K9 Beezley while Tollie rested.

Beezley promptly took us down the same driveway and at the same "T" she headed to the right, toward the highway. As we got close to the road, her head came up and she became extremely animated. She also stuck her head into a 50-foot-long culvert that led under the highway. Lynda joked that she better not be crittering on skunks. I thought I heard something, just like I had during a previous search over at the coast. This time I wasn't going to let it go as a ghost noise. And I wasn't so sure about her crittering either so shone my light into the pipe – it was only about two feet in diameter - but the beam couldn't reach the other side and nothing looked out of the ordinary. Beezley then crossed the Highway and we were met with a wall of blackberries. It was now terribly obvious that Beez was in strong scent of our missing person. Was she intwined in the berries? Our lights trying to penetrate the dark thorny brush. There it is, that noise again. Lynda turned around and saw the same drain pipe that I had looked into on the north side of the road.

Then I heard Lynda exclaim "she's in here!" Lauren was there. She was completely stuck in the culvert, about 20 feet from us.

She initially refused to leave the culvert but eventually she was coaxed out with a little assistance from friends. Other than some cuts and abrasions and being slightly dehydrated, confused and cold, she was going to be okay and was transported to the local hospital for treatment and observation.

*Lynda and K9 Beezley passing their*
*mission ready evaluation*

----------

I flanked for Lynda and K9 Beezley on several searches, one a human remains search in Siskiyou County in which K9 Beezley located what remained of the missing person. Let me just say, predation is a real thing. I also flanked for other members of the Unit when not working my dogs. One of those memorable experiences took place in the summer of 2016 back in California's Marble Mountains.

# The Long Hike Out

It was late June and Joseph Hopkins and his son Cody had been on a planned 10-day hiking trip through the Marble Mountains. They had planned to depart from Let'er Buck trailhead and finish their hike at Wooley Creek trailhead by 29 June. They never showed up at their final destination and a search was initiated the following day, a Thursday.

When the CORSAR callout came on Saturday afternoon, a specific request for wilderness air scent canines was made so Tollie was going to have to sit this one out. I was still responding, however, and offered to flank and support Denise and her dog, K9 Cody. Several other searchers from Josephine County joined the search as well. We all got

an early start in order to make the customary early morning briefing which was to take place at the at the Happy Camp/Oak Knoll Ranger Station. After Denise received her and K9 Cody's assignment the three of us then made our way to the small airfield at Happy Camp. Cody was a little nervous, he was

*Flying along the Klamath River enroute Pleasant Lake*

never a fan of uncontrollable movement, but settled down on the floor of the helicopter between Denise and myself. The exceptional California Highway Patrol Air crew of H-14 flew us down the Klamath River before turning east and rising over the Marble Mountains. They set us down with precision on a postcard size slab of granite at the east end of one of the prettiest lakes I've ever seen.

*Top: Being dropped off at Pleasant.*
*Below: Looking west toward the saddle we would hike over*

Pleasant Lake is a cirque lake and sits at 5,500 feet. On the west side of the lake were two rocky peaks of over 6,000 feet with a small saddle between them. To the east the land just fell away into Pleasant Valley. We made our way around the north shore of the lake noting the

campsite at the western edge of the lake hadn't been used in quite some time and then we navigated west up and over the saddle. We climbed up the rocky steep slope 400 feet before descending past an unnamed lake, through lush spring fed mountain meadows along a barely perceptible trail.

Cody was working ahead of us trying to catch a whisp of the missing. Just as we were about to intersect the Bridge Creek trail, Cody raised his head and with nose to the wind danced on his paws ahead of us, something had tickled his nose. The Bridge Creek trail is a little used 9.3-mile-long connector trail between the Wooley Creek trail in the south and the Haypress trail in the north. An internet trail report describes *"the Bridge Creek trail as traversing through the Bridge Creek Research Natural Area known for its botanical diversity of ancient conifers. This trail, however, is not maintained quite as much as other surrounding trails."* This trail seemed like a natural option for the Hopkin's to take in order to hook up with their planned itinerary. At the time, however, we weren't fully aware of trail names, conditions, where they led, the family's itinerary, or what had or hadn't been searched. We were just given an assignment. And it was not to proceed south along this faint trail but to head north toward the Haypress trail. That said, we both stood and watched Cody as he raised his head into the air. Which way would he want to go? When we intersected the barely discernable trail, I suggested we head south just a bit and see if we spot any footprints. We went only a short way and didn't see anything resembling a footprint. We turned around and headed north. There

*About to intersect the Bridge Creek trail. Cody, hidden in the tall grass, head held high in the air.*

233

really wasn't a clear trail to follow so we mostly just navigated using our map and compass and occasionally checked our GPS to make sure the terrain hadn't pulled us this way or that. As we climbed through brushy meadows, Cody flushed a huge deer from its thicket providing daytime concealment; being a good dog, he looked back at us but did not give chase. It was a heck of a climb for a warm day, from roughly 5,400 feet to over 6.400 feet to reach the ridgeline towering above us. The last portion was on granite scree and both Denise and I noticed that Cody was starting to struggle. The pads of his feet were being shredded by the abrasive decomposed granite, quartz, and general rocky underfoot found along most of our route. We stopped and dug through our packs and bandaged his feet best we could. It was clear, however, that he needed a ride out.

*Bill and I scouting the ridge for a potential helicopter landing zone*

Serendipitously, we met up with Bill and Traci from Josephine County at the top of the ridge. They had been airlifted into a bason of lakes just to the east known as the Cuddihy Lakes. Looking around on the ridge, we found what we thought was a suitable landing spot for the helicopter and then got on the radio and hoped they were available. We had confirmation that they were available and would attempt to land and pick up Denise and Cody but there were no guarantees. Traci decided to accompany Denise and Cody, which meant that Bill and I teamed up and headed onward to our next assignment. About 20 minutes later we heard the familiar sound of a helicopter approaching and listened to the radio communications confirming that everyone was safely aboard and heading back to base.

A report had come in that a group of campers might have seen the father and son. We were, therefore, tasked to perform an interview and possibly glean some clues about their possible whereabouts. The campers were at a place called Onemile Lake. Aptly named as the lake was one mile down a steep switchback trail into a lovely cirque just to our west. It was a 700-foot descent to the lake, the interview providing us

*On the trail to Onemile Lake. Still smiling so we must have been descending.*

no new information. Then it was a 700-foot climb back up to the ridgeline. It was getting late and we were instructed to hike back down the Haypress trail to the trailhead where a vehicle would be waiting for us. It was a long hike out and it was going to get dark. They instructed us that we really needed to be off the ridge, called Sandy Ridge, by nightfall due to the dangers of hiking that stretch after dark. The ridge runs for several miles and at 6,200 feet of elevation affords breathtaking unobstructed views to the west and the east. We took the hint though about trying to traverse it in the dark and we moved! I snapped pictures without stopping, the sun was setting fast. It was so dramatic and beautiful and one of those places where you feel small and inadequate. I loved it. We descended off the ridge just as the last rays of sunlight settled in for the long night.

*Looking east from Haypress Trail while hiking along Sandy Ridge*

We still had several miles of hiking to go. We were now deep in the forest. Our headlamps lighting the trail before us. All of a sudden Bill stopped and noted that according to his GPS we were no longer on the correct trail. He was sure that the terrain had pulled us down deeper into the forest and the correct trail was a couple hundred feet above us. I was pretty confident that we hadn't missed any turns and had experienced this before in the Marble Mountains. Plus, I wasn't keen on hiking back up the slope. I knew that trails and roads are not always depicted correctly on maps or on GPS systems and why relying on them can be troublesome. We were fine, I assured him and we continued on in the dark. A team of searchers from Jackson County, who were a few hours ahead of us and also hiking back to the same trailhead had flagged our left turn through the Let'er Buck Meadow where the Haypress, Stanshaw, and Let'er Buck trails all intersect. They could see that even in the daylight the turn through the wet meadow to stay on the Haypress and not get fooled into following another trail was not easy to spot. We were ever so thankful. If they hadn't flagged the turn, I am pretty sure we would have missed it. By now, my feet were really getting tired. I needed to stop and rest more frequently, Bill pushing me to continue. "We are almost there, just a few more miles." We were now following the narrow twisty Haypress Creek drainage that was off to our left. Bill stopped dead in his tracks again as his flashlight slipped from his hands and fell onto the trail. I literally bumped into him. Why had we stopped? Then I saw the eyes. Big golden eyes reflecting off our headlamps. The cougar was maybe 75 feet in front of us off to our left just standing on a log watching us. He looked curious; I was frightened. I had a bear bell on my pack and to this day I think the sound of my bell tinkering in the night brought out the curiosity of the cat. We got on the radio and let the team waiting at the trailhead, just a few corners away now, know what was going on. Celeste, the Siskiyou County SAR Coordinator, was listening to the radio traffic and asked us if we had an air horn with us. Bill and I chuckled to ourselves, nope forgot to pack the air horn. Then just as quick as the cat appeared it slipped into the night. The right side of the trail was steep with rock overhangs; we prayed the cat hadn't circled around behind us and gotten above us. We walked confidently but slowly down the trail. My feet didn't hurt anymore. We then heard a horn honking and the lights of a little white SAR jeep and Ted, good old reliable Ted at the helm! He had been waiting patiently for hours for us. It was after 1 am in the morning. I'd put a hard 16 miles on my feet and I was exhausted. After piling into the jeep, I think I managed to stay awake for about 15 minutes before falling fast asleep and not waking again until we were back at the SAR barn just as the first glimmers of light were breaking over the horizon.

The Hopkins father and son were found the next day, on Sunday July 4th. They set a signal fire which caught the attention of firefighters. Found in *"a remote drainage, a considerable distance from the initial search area. Both father and son were in relatively good shape considering their ordeal and they were reunited with family members shortly after their rescue,"* according to a press release from Siskiyou

County Sheriff's Office. By Wednesday, the signal fire was now named the "Wilderness Fire" and had burned 46 acres in the footprint of a 2008 fire; 18 smokejumpers were dispatched in addition to two hotshot crews to fight the blaze.

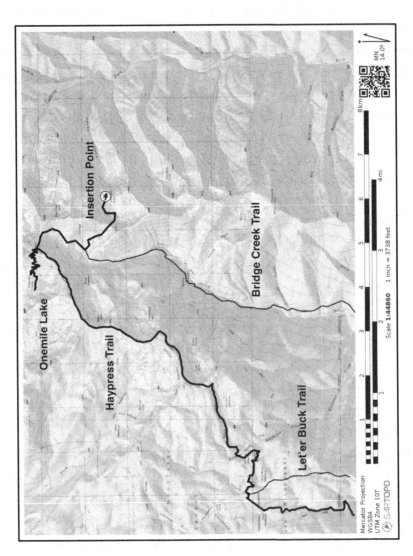

If Denise, K9 Cody, and I had stayed on the faint track to the left, instead of turning right when we intersected the Bridge Creek trail, and the terrain along the trail remained navigable we would have run straight into the duo. They were approximately six miles further down the trail and less than two miles from the southern terminus with the Wooley Creek trail.

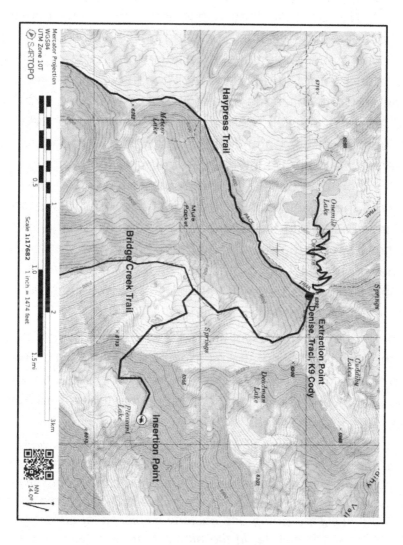

# Never Forget

Some searches just stick with you, they get stuck in your head, in your heart. Not because they concluded with "happy endings," but mostly because they did not. Someone got left behind. The Higgins search is one of those searches. It was also the first search that I made the hard decision not to respond when the initial call came. Our SAR Coordinator, Cory, called me on a stormy Friday night in October 2016 to alert me to a possible search the next morning for two overdue hunters up in the Bear Camp Ridge area. Bear Camp Ridge straddles the Josephine – Curry County border and runs southwest to northeast at an elevation of 4,800 feet. The ridge forms part of the southern boundary of the Shasta Costa Creek drainage. Jutting due north from Bear Camp Ridge into the drainage is a mile-long ridge called High Ridge; the view from the end of High Ridge provides a breathtaking view over one of the last un-protected roadless areas in our coastal mountains. I know this because I stood at the end of that trail in awe of what my eyes were privileged to witness.

On that Friday evening, October 14th, all of Oregon was bracing for one of the strongest wind storms in over a decade which was being fueled by remnants of Typhoon Songda. Meteorologists were projecting winds in excess of 100 miles an hour to pummel the coastal mountains, including Bear Camp Ridge.

*"Typhoon Songda, which at peak strength had 150 mph winds, was the twentieth named storm of the western Pacific typhoon season. During its journey north and east, Songda began to transform from a tropical typhoon to a storm system more associated with the mid-latitudes. As it did so, it hitched a ride on a particularly strong and easterly displaced jet stream (an area of narrow, strong winds high up in the atmosphere that helps to develop and*

*guide storm systems.) This strong jet stream directed the remnants of Songda directly at the Pacific Northwest."* (Tom Di Liberto, NOAA, October 28, 2016)

Being a bit of a weather junkie, I had been following the storms progress all day and with the forecasted projected winds and the search being high on a ridge, I told Cory that I just couldn't put myself or my dog into the woods under those conditions. It just wasn't going to be safe. Where had this sudden caution come from? I normally kind of "threw caution to the wind" but this time I said no. Afterall, these were experienced hunters and woodsmen and they assuredly would find a safe place to "hole up" for the night and then walk themselves out the next day. Saturday came and while the projected historic level windstorm didn't fully materialize it was still a forceful storm leaving thousands without power and trees down and roads flooded across the state. The other prediction that didn't occur was that the Higgins, father Shawn and son Trevor, did not walk out of the woods that Saturday.

*"On October 14, 2016, Shawn, his 21-year-old son Trevor, and Trevor's uncle were out hunting at the Shasta Costa drainage in the Bear Camp area about 45 miles east of Gold Beach, Oregon. Trevor and Shawn had gone their separate ways, but the plan was to meet back at the truck later that day and then drive to pick up Trevor's uncle who had been dropped off at another area of the woods earlier that day. Trevor, who had killed a buck the day before, was waiting at the truck for his dad, but he never showed up. He began to worry as it started to get dark and storm rolled in. As the hours passed, Trevor's uncle made it to the truck at the meeting place and the two of them split up to look for Shawn. But as it got darker, Trevor got turned around."* (Andrea Cavallier, October 11, 2020, ABC Dateline)

Although the winds diminished on Sunday, the rains certainly did not. Father and son had still not walked out and I couldn't in good conscience stay home a second day. Several of us from Josephine County dressed in our best rain gear and drove up into the mountains. Tollie and I rode up in Jeff's truck as I wasn't all that confident driving my Subaru along what was going to be a very wet and muddy track. Jeff was new to our K9 Unit and was training a lovely little redbone coonhound, Copper. We headed up to the very top of Bear Camp road (FSR 23), the infamous road the Kim family made a wrong turn off of and got so terribly lost 10 years ago. At the very top of Bear Camp road we made a sharp left turn on FSR 2308 locally referred to as the Burnt Ridge road. We followed this single-laned twisty, gravel and muddy track for several miles until we reached the command area which was set up just west of Squirrel Peak and High Ridge in a large landing.

*The Shasta Costa Creek Watershed from the High Ridge trail*

While the initial search area focused on the area the father and son had been hunting, the southern terminus of High Ridge, that ridge overlooked the vast Shasta Costa Creek watershed. The name derived from the Native American Indians who once inhabited the area. A map compiled in 1854 by J.L. Parish, an Indian Agent for the Port Orford District, reveals the drainage was utilized by a Tututni or Lower Rogue River Athabascan tribe called the Shasta Costa (also noted as Chasta Costa or Shas-te-koos-tees). Today, virtually all of this heavily forested area encompassing about 23,400 acres, lies within the Rogue River

Siskiyou National Forest. In 1996 an analysis of the watershed was conducted and it was found that half of the area could be categorized as late-successional habitat while over a third of the area was estimated to be old-growth forest with another fifteen percent of the forest considered mature. Fire suppression over the last century meant fuels had been accumulating on the forest floor and the meadows, places like Whitten Prairie, were slowly disappearing as the forest closed in on them. Ancient glacial activity had scoured the upper reaches of the watershed and in particular the area around Squirrel and Brandy Peaks, two of the prominent peaks within the search area leaving the slopes steep, very steep. Looking at a slope analysis map indicates that 50-90% slopes are common. I can confirm this. Established trails within the drainage are virtually non-existent. In fact, there is only one established trail and that is the Bear Camp Ridge trail (#1147) which extends for about 1.5 miles from the 23-2308 road intersection down Bear Camp Ridge to Elk Wallow road (road 2308-016). Forest Service maps also show another section of trail #1147 that parallels FSR 2308 and runs for about 2.5 miles from east of Brandy Peak west to about one mile east of Squirrel Peak. The trail the Higgin's were hunting along, which also paralleled the 2308 road is not depicted on the map. There is also a trail cut along the entire length of High Ridge. There are several historic trails which may or may not be evident in some places but are not depicted on any current maps.

We arrived at the command area early on Sunday morning in anticipation of getting a prompt start. We ran through the torrential driving rain, ducked under a pop-up, signed in and then we waited. And we waited. It was pouring rain so opted to wait in Jeff's truck and drink hot coffee. And we waited and waited some more. This was ridiculous. I didn't know the SAR manager on duty that day and knowing how busy

*Waiting and watching it rain*

it is for those planning and trying to conduct a search, especially under these challenging conditions, I didn't push them to hurry up. But no one from Josephine County was being deployed. Trevor and Shawn had been missing since Friday night and the more time that passed, the more contaminated the area becomes, the less chance there is of acquiring a trail. We sat and waited. Quality resources being wasted when every second counted. I absolutely hated this part of search and rescue. Some searches went off with military precision and other searches were a cluster. This one was starting out like a cluster. It wasn't until 1430 in the afternoon that I was finally in the field. And the assignment was all wrong.

I was assigned to work my trailing dog in Area D with Jeff as my support and three ground searchers (Brett, Heather, and Roger) from Josephine County. This was maybe an assignment for an air scent dog but not for a trailing dog. Area D was an area of about 300 x 1000 meters in size or approximately 75 acres. Trying to make the best of the situation, I broke our team up and the ground searchers did a Type II search of Area D. A Type II search or loose grid search is characterized as a fast systematic search of a high probability area and assumes the missing subject is alive and responsive.

My plan was to work Tollie as a trailing dog as best I could within the limitations of our assignment. Two scent articles – a ballcap and a pillowcase – were made available or the K9 teams. I used a 2 x 2 piece

244

of gauze and carefully placed the gauze in the bag containing both the ballcap and the pillowcase bag to transfer the scent of both of the missing to the piece of cotton. One piece of luck was that Area D contained both the point-last-seen and the last-known-point of the missing. The rain continued to fall in buckets, the west wind blowing it near horizontal at times and the temperature never broke the 40-degree mark. It was miserable. We were done with our assignment before 4 pm. A quick synopsis taken directly from my search report:

Scented my K9 as planned and began searching the northern section of Area D. The other ground personnel searched in a grid pattern below me making two passes through Area D. As we started out, K9 Tollie headed up toward a ridge and in the direction of Squirrel Peak. We noted footprints and flagging as we proceeded. K9 Tollie, on occasion was checking vegetation for scent. We continued further east than our assigned area because K9 Tollie was working methodically and with intent and wanted to continue in the direction toward Squirrel Peak. After about 500 feet, I turned him around and we cleared the center of Area D.

During the standard debrief at the completion of an assignment, I did make note of something that struck me as "odd." Again, from my original search report:

While in the search area, it struck me as "odd" that you had to descend to go back to the road which intuitively is along a ridge itself. The terrain itself was pulling us up and over Squirrel Peak. Based on field and search experience, I suggest the drainage on the east side of Squirrel Peak (the Squirrel Camp Creek Drainage) would be a good place to search.

I was so frustrated at the end of the day that I chose not to return on Monday. I did return Tuesday as a ground searcher and led a team of trained SAR members and emergent volunteers to clear a parcel of land. While we turned up nothing, another ground team working down Squirrel Camp Creek Drainage area located Trevor Higgins. Alive! He was found along the creek approximately 2.5 miles below the ridge. A US Coast Guard helicopter flew in to attempt to airlift Trevor from the drainage. The skies were mostly cloudy, the winds swirly in the rugged terrain, this was not going to be easy. And just like magic, the clouds opened up just enough for the delicate hoist maneuver to happen.

*"Curry County Sheriff John Ward says Trevor Higgins was quite scared when searchers found him at the Shasta Costa drainage. "He was very hypothermic, very cold, he was alert," Sheriff John Ward said.*

*But he thinks he will a make a full recovery. Trevor was sent to a Coos Bay hospital suffering from hypothermia even though he used fire to keep himself warm.*

*Meanwhile, the search for Shawn in what Sheriff John Ward calls one of the most vast and rugged areas in Curry County continues at daylight."* (KOBI5 News, October 16th, 2016)

The search for Trevor's father Shawn continued for another week and then the hard decision was made to end the search. Sheriff Ward told media outlets at the time:

*"It is with a heavy heart that we have to suspend the search for Shawn at this time. Our hearts go out to the family, friends and community that love Shawn so dearly. We pray that they will find a way to makes sense of this tragedy and heal their hearts. The connection that the people of Coos County have with each other and the way they come together to help each other is nothing but astonishing and an example for other communities to live by. I am very humbled."*

The official search ended on Tuesday Oct 25th. I never went back during the official ground search efforts after Trevor was airlifted out of the wilderness. I'm not really sure why. That doesn't mean, however, that I ever forgot.

The truth is I did go back, twice. Onetime on an official mission and onetime off the record. The first time was on Friday of the same week that the massive ground search concluded. This next phase of the search effort was part of a special human remains detection search effort with handlers from all around the region participating. I brought Beryl with me but I knew at her age she would not be able to search in this rugged terrain but there still might be a small role for her to play. Better to have her along than at home, I figured. My main job that day was to support Lynda and K9 Beezley. Our assignment was to walk out the High Ridge trail to its terminus. Other teams were scattered in treacherous drainages and or navigating steep slopes.

As we started along High Ridge heading north, K9 Beezley kept head checking or running out to the east into the Squirrel Camp Creek drainage. Every time she ran east or did one of these huge head checks, we both instinctively took a bearing on the wind and the

direction of the run outs and jotted the information down on a notepad. As we reached the terminus of the High Ridge trail, we stopped for a midday break. In between bites on a granola bar, I started plotting all the information we had collected on our map. Many of the lines crossed. Where they

*The rugged Squirrel Camp Creek drainage*

crossed, I drew a big "X." We both stared at the map and we decided we needed to get down into the drainage below and try and search around the "X." We were at 4,850 feet sitting at the end of the High Ridge Trail and our "X" was 1,000 feet below. We managed to descend only 200 feet before the near vertical slopes became treacherous. The afternoon drew on, with each foot step we had to weigh our options. We never got to our "X." It was late in the afternoon when we finally returned to base. There was, however, other activity going on.

In addition to the HRD canines searching that day, there was a private party using what we were told was some undisclosed proprietary technology to search the forest from the air above. I believe it was an attempt to use eDNA to capture the DNA of Shawn. This secretive group even went so far as to collect soil samples at a couple of locations because their device reportedly indicated there was DNA of Shawn in the soil. To me this was an expensive wild goose chase that preyed on the families hope of finding their missing loved one. After the soil was collected, the canine handlers were asked to "run their dogs over the samples to see if they sniffed any remains." The samples were placed alongside the road just into the vegetation. I rolled my eyes and was not going to participate; I just hung back and watched from a distance. I watched and believe to this day that I observed two experienced handlers cue their dogs into giving their trained final response. I shook my head and then decided "okay, I'll play along." Was I biased going in to this exercise? Absolutely, I thought it was ridiculous and dangerous. I also trusted Beryl and was pretty darn sure she wasn't going to "alert" on any of these jars. She had been sitting in her crate most of the day and this would be a perfect little exercise for her. I popped her out of the vehicle, harnessed her up and grabbed my long line. When I gave her the search cue, I purposely began her search away from the samples and on the opposite side of the road from any of the jars. We then crossed the road. She noticed the jars and stuck her nose deep into each jar and moved on without a care in the world. When my SAR Coordinator asked me for my impressions, I strongly suggested this type of exercise not be conducted the way it was setup. It was fraught with potential bias and with the family present it just left a very bad taste in my mouth. In my report, I suggested:

**IF** this is repeated, one person places the jars to be checked for HRD in a line with several other jars with similar material. That person will not watch the dogs work and only that person will know "the answer." This will at least make the process more in line with a double-blind test and will reduce the possibility of handler cuing and bias.

We left that evening as the sun set and the fog rolled from the ocean and over the mountain ridge. How did I end up leading everyone out? I couldn't see a thing. Jeff, who rode with me today, reminded me several times that the road was narrow and there was a cliff to his right. I peered through the pea soup fog as best I could, driving at a snail's pace. As we hit the pavement, the fog started to lift and we drove home mostly silent in the dark.

----------

This search from beginning to end was just plain frustrating for me and for several of us really. It was 11 months later, in the early fall of 2017 that a handful of us (myself, Dave, Jeff, Bill, Lynda and K9 Beezley) went for a walk down into Squirrel Camp Creek drainage in order to try and reach the "X."

This, of course, was an unofficial search effort but I know others that continued to go back up to the Bear Camp Ridge area after the search officially ended to keep looking. To keep looking for Shawn. To keep looking for some clue of what happened. His firearm was never located, for example. I had studied the search maps for hours and plotted us a route that I

*Unofficial Search Group: Jeff, myself, Bill, Lynda, Dave, and K9 Beezley*

believed was going to be the least treacherous way down into the drainage. We slowly made our way down and by midday we reached the "X" depicted on the map. We searched the area as best as the terrain allowed but came up empty. We did find a plastic bag, probably

249

left behind from the original search effort, we found some animal bones, but no firearm and no clues. We then crawled our way back up through the dense vegetation to the High Ridge trail and back to the safety of the road and our vehicles. While we didn't find a thing, we all felt like we searched well and that we were able to put the frustrations of the search, especially that first day, behind us. Searchers need closure too.

*Searching the steep Squirrel Camp Creek drainage near the "X"*

----------

What do I think happened? I still think Shawn remains down in the Squirrel Camp Creek drainage. It was easy to believe when you were on the High Ridge trail that you were on the trail that paralleled the FSR 2308 road and you had to descend to reach the road. Where those two trails met was brushy and confusing. If you made this mistake, your instincts would pull you unsuspecting into the Squirrel Camp Creek drainage. Trevor got turned around and ended up far down the drainage. I suspect the same thing happened to his father. With a storm coming in that night and being unprepared to spend a night out, he probably made a shelter or found a hollow log or some other sheltered spot, there were rock outcroppings peppered throughout the area, to hole up in through the storm. There is the possibility that hypothermia, a fall, being hit by a falling tree or branch, or a combination of all these possibilities is what finally led to Shawn not coming home.

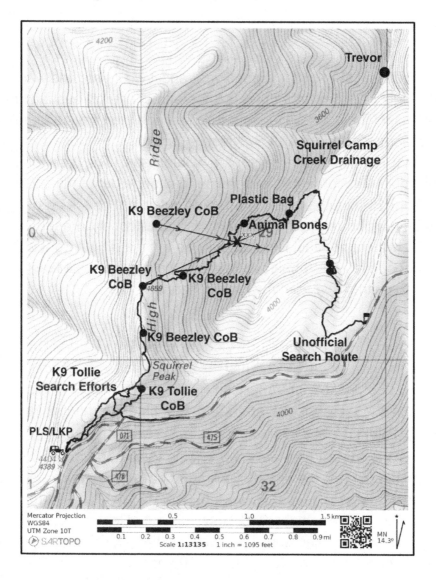

# The Race Against Time

2017 did not start out as a good year and it would not end well either. As the new year dawned, however, the sun shone on beautiful freshly fallen snow. The dogs played and frolicked and then settled for naps on their hammock beds that were nestled against the house to take full advantage of the warm rays of a winter sun. They all looked so comfortable and content. I went inside to change out of my snow pants and about 15 minutes later I went back outside to check on everyone. Winston was on his hammock with his head loosely draped over the side. He was gone. Just like that, he had left me. I never got a chance to say goodbye. Oh Winnie, you always were a loner. At least I had a search to distract me from my broken heart.

----------

The search was over in Curry County in the Emily Creek Drainage. I had been here once before just as my search career was getting started. I had flanked for Janet and her bloodhound, K9 Angie, before being assigned to a ground team and spending the day fighting brush and side hilling across steep slopes.

I knew the roads in the area were going to be poor so Jeff, who was going to support myself and K9 Tollie that day, drove us over in one of the little white SAR jeeps. It was January 12th and the weather was projected to be in the high 30's to low 40's but at least the sun was out. It had been raining and snowing since Sokhan Oul had gone missing, two days prior. She was Cambodian, 70 years old, only 4'10" tall, and maybe weighed 100 pounds. She was reported to be dressed in dark-coloured clothes and wore only light weight tennis shoes. She had been harvesting mushrooms when she went missing. She was not dressed or prepared for the wintery conditions.

I received another odd assignment but this time I questioned it and I diplomatically suggested to command that I start in the discipline for which my K9 was trained, mantrailing, and then I promised that if we couldn't find a scent trail that I would try and "do a wide area search of the area." There were a few wilderness air scent teams on scene that day but apparently not enough for all the boxes they had drawn on the master search map. We would acquiesce and search a box if nothing else materialized.

I needed a scent article to even start, however, and one of the air scent teams was requesting a scent article as well. Accompanied by Josephine County Deputy Stanton, we drove approximately 5 miles back down the mountain to the subject's camping location in order to collect a scent article. I used a 2 x 2 scent transfer taken from the seat crack of her car seat. The other K9 handler proceeded to do the same and then we coached Deputy Stanton how to collect extra scent articles in case any other canine handlers requested one.

From the 1107 road, a 4 x 4 jeep road – narrow, rutted and muddy – led to the point-last-seen; Jeff drove us delicately downhill until the track we were on intersected yet another small jeep road and parked. I scented K9 Tollie while he remained in the vehicle as per my usual routine. When I clipped the long line onto Tollie's harness, he popped out of the vehicle and immediately went to work. It was 1020 in the morning. Tollie first checked the jeep road we had just come down in both directions and then checked the other jeep road but gave a negative indication in all three directions. "No trail here," he said.

There was a small game trail that left the road almost opposite of where we had parked; we assumed this was most likely the way into the woods used by the family hunting for mushrooms. Tollie decided this must be the way also and headed into the woods on the little trail.

He then began working southward staying just below a ridgeline. After contouring along the slope for approximately one-third of a mile we intersected a north-south running dirt track (the same jeep road we had driven down earlier). With little hesitation, Tollie confidently turned south. It was about this time that we began hearing reports that the on-

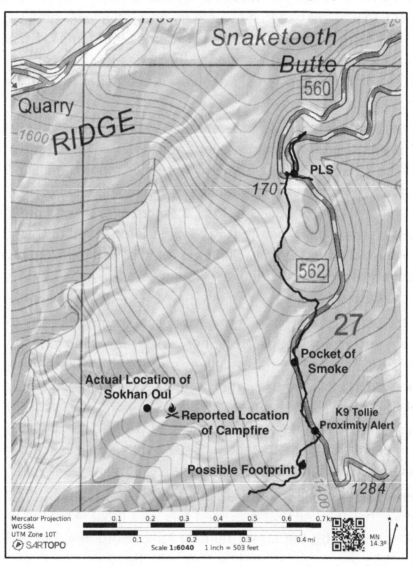

scene helicopter had spotted smoke from a possible signal fire. As we proceeded down the dirt-track we were able to mark into our GPS the location that the helicopter had seen smoke (10T 408096E 4666196N). The time was stamped as 10:51:34 AM. We radioed into command that we believed K9 Tollie was in scent and was showing strong trailing behaviour and most notably we had just worked through a pocket of light smoke that we could barely visibly discern but we could definitively smell. We also were in radio contact with Team 7 who had started to move quickly toward the coordinates provided by the helicopter. Since Ground Team 7 was going direct to coordinates we did not divert from K9 Tollie's task of following and working the subject's scent. What if she was not at the reported campfire but had moved? We needed to stay on task and focused on the scent trail. We continued for another tenth of a mile when K9 Tollie turned abruptly 90 degrees to the right and

headed straight up through dense brush to crest the ridge line. We spotted a possible footprint in the mud in thick brush. K9 Tollie begin exhibiting behaviour that he was in "proximity" scent of the subject. Tollie was working the scent pool and he turned back northwest pulling with such purpose; I was barely holding on as my little brown bear expertly and quickly negotiated the forest. My goal was to just remain upright. Over the radio came the fantastic news, that Team 7 had made the locate. At the time we were approximately 1000 feet from subject's reported location (10T 408021E 4666204N). The time

*Sokhan Oul thanking Sheriff John Ward*

was 11:19:15 AM. I had a few friends on Team 7 and we often joke among ourselves how it became a bit of a race and that the long legs of the ground searchers were quicker on this day than the nose of the canine.

It was amazing good news as Sokhan was alive and well. She was a smoker and had been able to make a fire to keep her warm while she huddled her body against the elements. When search teams safely got her back to Command, before she ate anything she thanked all the searchers and checked to make sure they were all eating and being cared for before she sat down to eat anything.

----------

I needed this feeling of accomplishment coming so soon after losing Winston. This good feeling about the search helped get me through the toughest year of my life.

# Final Chapters

We held many of our K9 Unit trainings at two Bureau of Land Management seed orchards that we had been given special access, even though the sites were closed to the public. In March, we were training at the Sprague Seed Orchard when both Tollie and I picked up and were eventually bitten by small ticks. Ticks were a common nuisance whenever we were out in the field. During the days' training we had a callout and so we packed up from training and headed down to O'Brien for a human remains search. It would be Beryl's last deployment. She was just shy of 13 years old. As we searched, I felt the familiar sting as the tick bite me but was too lazy to drop my pants and pluck it off my leg. Dang, it really hurt.

The next day I woke up and could barely walk. This had never happened before. I also noticed that Tollie had thrown up sometime during the night. He didn't feel well all weekend, drinking but not really eating and he threw up a couple more times. By Monday he was really sick and I called the vet as soon as they opened and said I was bringing him in. He was miserable and shaking as if pain, and that morning had started throwing up bile. When I arrived at the vet clinic, they quickly took him into the back to run tests. It was going to be awhile so I drove home and waited with trepidation by the phone. They called only a short time later with the devasting news, "He's experiencing kidney failure." "What? How could this be? Was he going to be okay?" They weren't sure he was going to make it, they had him on fluids to flush his system and had started him on antibiotics. I quickly drove back to the vet clinic. For five days Tollie was in intensive care and on IV fluids. Round the clock care. I consulted with a vet friend of mine who also owns Sussex and she was not optimistic that he would be okay. I was devasted. I made a visit to the local emergency clinic to get myself checked out and was put on doxycycline for my tick bite as the bite area and my entire leg was now swollen and painful. I checked with the seed orchard to ascertain if they were using any chemicals anywhere on the property; they reported back and assured me that there were none on site. By the end of the week, I was allowed to bring Tollie home and we would just monitor him closely. He was put on a special food, but after looking at the ingredients, and spending hours online and sifting through copious amounts of literature, opinions, and the like, I ditched the processed kidney food and opted to cook for him instead. He slowly improved. While all of this was transpiring, poor FOD was really having a hard time.

Winston's brother FOD (FOD stands for Foreign Object Damage, an aviation term) was really showing signs of being almost 15-years-old although he still trundled along on our daily walks around the property. He had cognitive decline and for what seemed like a year or so he would wake up in the night and howl or just wander around confused. I tried every trick in the book, needless to say I hadn't had a good night's sleep in a long time. Toward the beginning of April, I noticed a growth in his mouth that was only getting larger. I thought maybe it was another ranula, he had experienced those a couple of times previously, but this growth was different. My favorite vets were out of town and the other vet in the clinic couldn't get a good look at the growth when I took him in for an assessment. One day while walking through the kitchen he bit down on the growth and blood spurt everywhere. I knew this wasn't going to get better. Dave wanted to take him back to the vet and I knew that if we did, he wouldn't be coming home with us. I finally found the courage to make the appointment and we took FODdie to the vet for the last time. He needed to be sedated as we said our tearful goodbyes. He was one week shy of his 15th birthday. I discovered that his and

Winston's littermate, Lucy, had passed around Christmas time. My entire first litter of Sussex pups from Connie were all were gone within four months of each other. Things were only to get worse. Beryl would be gone by year's end.

Tollie improved but his desire for the work never returned in full. Some days he seemed just like the old Tollie but other days he seemed tired. To be fair, I was having similar feelings. The Puck Lake search was one of the good days for both of us.

*Left to Right: Conne, Beryl, Winston, Tollie, FOD*

# Puck Lake

If the search location had been anywhere else but the Sky Lakes Wilderness, I probably would have declined the callout. I hadn't yet spent much time in the Sky Lakes but it's lakes and trails had always intrigued me. It was the beginning of August which meant souring temperatures in our inland valleys and that would be too much stress on Tollie's system. But this search was at about 6,000 feet of elevation and the temperatures were only going to be in the mid-70's that day. The skies weren't even close to blue, with wildfire smoke in the air, but the smoke wasn't of the choking variety either. It was gearing up to be a good day to get out of the heat and get a peek into a wilderness I had always wanted to visit.

*The smoke-filled skies over Puck Lake*

The day before, Steven Ivey and his partner had gone for a day hike into Puck Lake from the Nannie Creek trailhead. When it was time to return to their vehicle, they split up each taking a different route around the lake. His wife, if I recall, returned to the lake to search for her husband but didn't find Steven along the trail system. She then called search and rescue. Steven was 63 years old and wearing green and natural coloured clothing and carried only a small day pack. He had little to no wilderness experience. Klamath County SAR members spent most of the night searching and made "voice contact" with him on the northwest side of Puck Lake. Sound plays tricks in the mountains and the SAR team failed to locate Steven.

That following morning searchers from several counties arrived on scene to assist, including myself and Tollie. We were the only K9 team on scene that morning. I was assigned a support person from Klamath County; Lou was his name. I had never worked with him before, but jotted down in my notebook after the search that he could flank for me anytime.

My assignment was to see if I could find his trail, or ideally Steven, in the area where the ground team that morning had heard his voice. That had been at 0700. It was now 1130. It was a hike of about 3 miles from the trailhead to the area northwest of Puck Lake. I collected a scent article from the passenger side of the subject's jeep, the reporting party made mention that she had driven that day and Steven had ridden as the passenger. Like I often did, I scented Tollie prior to arriving at the either the point-last-seen or the last-known-point since we could come across scent clues anywhere between search base and our assigned area. Steven, for example, could be still be making his way back to the trailhead. In fact, we hadn't hiked far when Tollie gave a very strong head-check into a north-south running draw that sloped steeply off the right-hand side of the trail. It was indicative of what he did when he hit scent. He even tried to leave the trail. I made a note of the location and wind direction which not surprisingly was upslope right into his nose. Knowing that these scent pockets can be caried quite a distance on the wind or settle into pockets made by the terrain, again quite a distance from the lost person, I chose to continue to the location where we had a confirmed clue: voice contact. On the north end of Puck Lake, we met up with ground Team 3. They were heading back to command so I briefed them on our scent clue and suggested they keep their eyes peeled when they got to that portion of the trail.

We then headed off to the area northwest of the lake where our search assignment was to begin. Tollie seemed to pick up a scent trail quickly and proceeded in a northerly direction. We eyed a possible footprint which also seemed to point north. Then at 10T 566777 4721009, 6493 ft, 2:05:19 PM K9 Tollie gave a strong indication of acquiring a nose full of scent.

We were now side hilling across a dry forested slope, to the left was up, to the right was down. The wind was upslope and from the east. Tollie continued to head check down into the draw. It felt like we were running on the high side of scent so we proceeded down toward Threemile Drainage. I felt confident enough of what Tollie was trying to convey that I relayed what was happening back to command. When we reached the bottom of the slope, Tollie started was intently working a dry-creek bed. At 10T 567868 4721011, 6230 ft, 2:54:53 PM K9 Tollie again gave another strong indication of intercepting and acquiring another nose full of scent.

We noted that the two indications were in line with each other and followed along a dry feeder creek that led to Threemile Creek proper. Tollie pulled us south and then he turned east along another dry creek bed; at this time, I removed the lead due to thick brush and steeper and rockier terrain. Tollie continued pulling us east. We took a short break, studied the map, and discussed our options. We believed that we needed to continue further east along the line of scent clues and the

Left: Tollie on the hike back to Puck Lake.    Right: Scree slope on north side of MT6607

direction Tollie was working. As we studied the map, however, we noted a significant and steep drop-off lied just ahead of us. We then had to take an honest assessment of the terrain, our physical status (all three of us were beginning to be a bit tired) and the time of day and we ultimately made the tough decision to hike up back toward Puck Lake. Unknown to us, we were only about 2,000 feet as the crow flies from Steven when we took our break. After we turned around and hiked south, Tollie lost the scent he had been trying to source. We continued back to base by taking a short cut to clear a small knoll. As we approached that same draw we encountered on the hike into Puck Lake, the one leading to the north, Tollie again gave indications of scent being down in the draw.

It was 1730 by the time we finally returned to base. Tollie had worked for five hours and had covered some 11 miles. After getting Tollie some water and making sure he was resting comfortably back in his crate I headed over to the utility trailer to be debriefed. Graham, an experienced searcher in addition to being experienced in the various command roles, started asking me the standard questions and filling out the requisite paperwork. We then started plotting on the electronic

263

master map the changes of behaviour that Tollie exhibited and then he asked me to point out where I recommended further search efforts be focused. I pointed to a spot on the map and we were in the midst of

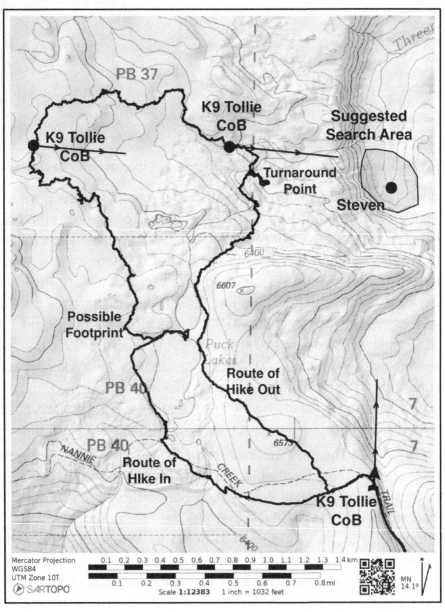

drawing that circle on the map when the radio buzzed to life with the word that the private air asset, the now infamous John Rachor, had spotted the subject waving a white T-shirt and to stand by for coordinates. As Graham plotted those coordinates on the electronic map I watched as they fell right in the center of where we were drawing my circle. We looked at each other and smiled.

----------

Maybe Tollie was going to be okay and regain that spark that I thought he had lost. A couple weeks later there was a search for a presumed drowning victim on the Rogue River near Indian Mary Park. I brought Tollie along. He didn't have a lot of boat experience but maybe an opportunity would arise where he could be of some assistance. He had just been certified in human remains detection. The dive team had the inflatable rubber boat (IRB) out and were just doing some preliminary river scans. Could Tollie jump aboard? Sure. As we waited in the front of the boat, Terry, our boat driver who loved to work with the dogs, came bounding down the boat ramp to hop in and get us moving. Tollie became frightened and started to bark and as Terry grabbed the side of the IRB to push the boat back and simultaneously jump into the boat Tollie grabbed his arm. I was mortified. I said we would leave immediately but Terry backed the boat away and into the river. Tollie settled down and went to work sniffing the air; he wasn't experienced like Beryl but was working okay. We stopped once along a sandy bank so Heather, who was with us, could make a pit stop and Tollie and I exited the boat and then we got into the boat last to avoid anyone coming toward him before pushing off again. We finished up the morning and I immediately reported the incident to our SAR Coordinator, Cory. I made yet another veterinary appointment for him. This time it was a bad ear infection. We took some time off. We went backpacking in the Mountain Lakes with Lynda and Beezley, Lynda's son and his dog. It was nice just being in the wilderness and actually not searching but just enjoying the beauty around me.

Tollie searched one last time that year a few days after I said goodbye to Beryl. A bunch of friends who were employed to work in one of the marijuana fields had gone for a day in the mountains and accidently left one of their friends behind. Tollie worked fine, road happily in the back of a SAR rig with other searchers, but I realized I was emotionally and mentally spent. Losing Beryl had broken more than my heart it seemed. My spirit had been broken as well.

*Tired but happy after a long day out on the hunt*

SAR K9 Tollie

Quarr Tollard Royal, SAR-W, TDCH, NCO-1, NCOT-1

(May, 3 2012 – )

# Postscript

Losing three of my dogs in one year, almost losing Tollie, and then the constant worry about his health was just too much. At the Christmas

Party that year I received the coveted Jim Clarke Award. This award is given to the search and rescue volunteer for *"Outstanding Dedication and Commitment to the Citizens of Josephine County through Participation in the Josephine County's Sheriff Office Search and Rescue Division."* It seemed perhaps a fitting way to maybe end a career? My logs show that we participated in one more search, a human remains search in early January 2018. My logs also showed I stopped keeping logs. I officially handed over "the reigns" of the K9 Unit to Lynda. I was still training with everyone, just not as regularly. I was also one of the primary academy trainers for our new search and rescue recruits teaching land navigation and search tactics. Two topics that I loved. The training coordinator, who coincidently was also the same canine handler that I had had such a falling out with, made it clear that other SAR personnel should be given the opportunity to teach those topics. With that responsibility now stripped from me, I was really seeing no reason to continue. Another loss after a year of losses was just too much.

I spent most of that drier than average winter reflecting and trying to heal by hiking with Tollie in the local mountains. About half of each hike was spent off trail navigating through the woods with just a map and compass. I suppose I was trying to get as close to the earth as possible, sometimes taking little chances in order to just feel something again. That spring, Tollie got sick with yet another mysterious infection. During this time my husband had enquired if I was contemplating perhaps getting another puppy? Maybe he noticed I was struggling. Initially I wasn't sure but maybe, just maybe, a new puppy would brighten my spirits. In May, I welcomed Millie into my heart. Millie is a working cocker spaniel from some amazingly well-bred working lines.

I was actually really excited to start teaching her. She is cute and spunky, full of joy. and while not a Sussex, she is still brown. After her inoculations were complete, I drove to a scheduled canine training up at Myers Camp, one of my favorite training spots in the Briggs Valley. Millie did some baby tracks and small article searches and wowed everyone with her cuteness and smartness. I also ran a trail with Tollie. As I battled the brush, something I'd done countless times before, I said "no more." I was truly done. Even a puppy couldn't mend the heartache and losses of the previous year.

It took me well over a year to officially turn in my gear. During that time, I don't recall going out on any searches or doing any regular SAR training. I just let Tollie rest and Millie and I just played together without the pressures of search and rescue. Millie loved to track and quickly earned her Tracking Dog and her Variable Surface Tracking titles from the American Kennel Club. I was also honing her detection skills and we took a mock article-evidence detection test in the spring of 2021 which she passed easily. I also joined a local spaniel group and I rekindled my love of gundog work. I started to teach online under the name *SeekingScent*, my classes focusing on precision hard surface tracking, detection, and gundog foundations. I also was teaching in person agility classes at a local training center. I was keeping busy.

Leaving SAR would be one of the toughest conclusions to arrive at. I came home from a trip to the United Kingdom where I had attended a conference, given a presentation on skills for SAR dogs and their handlers, and delivered a beginning tracking workshop with the realization that it was time for new adventures. In November 2019, after nearly 15 years of being on call 24/7, I officially retired from Josephine County Search and Rescue.

----------

*K9 Millie*

A mere month and a half after leaving Josephine County SAR, the world would change forever. A deadly pandemic encircled the globe with millions dying; it lasted through 2021 and restrictions on movement were only fully eased in 2022. I spent those two years trying to write this book and made it about half way through when it ground to a halt. It was just too hard to write. I was having fun teaching and coaching students from around the world as we all learned to navigate and stay connected through Zoom. Once travel restrictions were lifted, I travelled to

Australia to share my knowledge, much of it gained directly from my SAR experiences, with handlers wanting to learn more about tracking. I would on occasion meet up with my old SAR friends and train Millie or help them with a struggle. I even provided some special bespoke training and assisted with OSSA K9 evaluations.

In the spring of 2022 after much thought and reflection, I rejoined Josephine County SAR albeit in a much more limited capacity. Millie officially certified in article-evidence detection and for in-county human remains detection. She's been on a few searches and performed well. I'm not sure what our future holds within SAR; while the passion remains the burning fire within me has admittingly dwindled. In 2023, I turned 60 years old and decided that I better finish this book, this chapter of my life.

Climb every mountain,
Search high and low,
Follow every byway,
Every path you know.
Climb every mountain,
Ford every stream,
Follow every rainbow,
'Til you find your dream.
A dream that will need
All the love you can give,
Every day of your life
For as long as you live.

Oscar Hammerstein II

After retiring from a near twenty-year career with the US Government, Ann and her husband, Dave, decided to make southern Oregon their home. Not being an idle type, Ann joined Josephine County Search and Rescue in the winter of 2005 and the K9 Unit the following year. In addition to working her own canines, she coached and assisted other canine team members during her time as the Unit lead. She also was a SAR Academy Instructor and trained and served in a Command Role. While still active in SAR, Ann devotes much of her time to teaching, coaching, and inspiring student from across the globe in all disciplines of search work via on-line platforms. Ann also travels on occasion to present in-person workshops. In her spare-time she enjoys hiking and photographing wild flowers in the mountains of southern Oregon, often accompanied by a brown dog or two. She and her husband are also active members of the Cascade Region Porsche Club where they plan and lead spirited drives along the area's beautiful mountain roads.

Made in the USA
Las Vegas, NV
04 February 2024

85300806R00163